# Sharia Exposed

## Farzana Moon

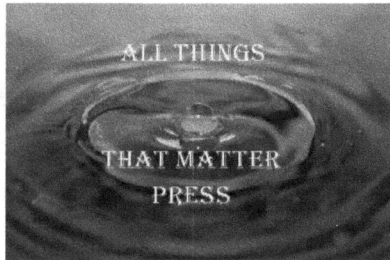

ISBN 13: 9780996663458

Library of Congress Control Number: 2016936589

Cover design by All Things That Matter Press

Published in 2016 by All Things That Matter Press

For Amat-un-Nur my spiritual guide and teacher

# Foreword

*Thus we put you on the right way of religion. So follow it and follow not the whimsical desire of those who have no knowledge.* (Quran 45:18)

Though Sharia as a legal code didn't exist during the lifetime of the Prophet Muhammad, many scholars believe that this verse above is the only sharia verse in the Quran. Sharia literally means the straight path, or right way of religion. Against countless definitions of Sharia, the simplest one in the literal sense of the word is: a way to the watering place and path to seek felicity and salvation.

This book deals with basic Sharia, the Quranic verses which have become the tools of tyranny in the hands of the zealots. These tools are rough-hewn, ingrained with the rust of distortions. In order to take that rust off, one needs to polish them with reason, interpreting what is misinterpreted. Then lending them the sheen of purity from the Quranic verses which need no interpretation since they are the embodiment of love, peace and harmony by the very essence of their candid rhythm in poetry and simplicity. In this book, first and foremost, Sharia would gather the most neglected of gems from the Quran and the Hadiths which radiate love, peace and compassion before ripping open the fabrication of the verses which have become the weapons of war, hate and intolerance. Sharia is much like the present day GPS of path-finding through byways and highways to reach a certain destination, depending upon the goals of each individual. Sharia as Islamic Law defined by the traditions of the Prophet recorded in Hadiths as Sunnah and through the Quranic revelations, is in sore need of being scrubbed clean of distortions to avoid the road blocks, where the ancient streets of redundant knowledge are overgrown with weeds and the construction of new streets have nothing new to offer, exposed to the need to demolish and reconstruct.

The revelations were sacred tools of problem solving during the lifetime of the Prophet Muhammad dealing with specific situations which needed immediate attention. Islamic GPS of Sharia/Sunnah in twenty-first century is groping its way out of the labyrinth of time to shed its weight of human understanding, of man-made judgments and recollections, resulting in volumes upon volumes of traditions. More than three fourths of which have nothing to do with the life of the Prophet or his sayings, but with the need to control, subjugate, and manipulate each and every aspect of life under the pretense of religion as viewed by the so-called Islamic caliphs, jurists, scholars, historians and theologians.

First of all, Sharia as in the Quran and Hadith is to be taken into account and its layers of distortion, interpretation and fabrication peeled off slowly and gradually to reveal the purity of Islam which lies ensconced under the man-made laws of tyranny—those laws still vague and indecipherable. To explain, discuss, and disseminate in simple terms the Law of Islam without the weight of Arabic and unfamiliar terms is the aim of this book. It strives to reach young Muslims in this modern world so that they can explore and understand Islam in all its aspects of morality and universality. One of the most commonly used term by the Muslim scholars, Fiqh, is also avoided in this book for the benefit of easy-read and clear understanding. Fabrication of Sharia by Fiqh—human understanding of Sharia and its interpretation is the theme of this book, aiming toward exploring the past and the present for a better future.

Paradoxically, most of the Muslim writers neglect to portray the core values of Islam as love, peace and harmony, instead molding the Quranic revelations into the bullets of zeal, orthodoxy and intolerance. They focus more on the mundane, what to wear, what to eat, who to befriend, than on the important values of courtesy, kindness, tolerance. The same is true of the most of the Islamic publishers who shun the true precepts of Islam, rejecting authentic works in favor of the ones replete with man-made interpretations of holy revelations to promote edicts harsh and intolerable.

Nowhere in the Quran it is mentioned that women are not allowed to seek knowledge, or banned from working, or forbidden to leave their homes. On the contrary, in the Hadith, Traditions of the Prophet as Sunnah, the Prophet says, "The Pursuit of knowledge is a divine commandment for every Muslim male and female."

In utter ignorance of the Islamic spirit Malaysia has banned the use of the name of Allah by non-Muslims. To burst the bubble of piety for those of zeal who have issued such an edict, they need to know that Allah is an Arabic name for God Lord of the Worlds.

Allah was the God of Abraham, of Moses, of Jesus, of Muhammad, even of the pagan Arabs who knew that Kaaba was dedicated to one unknown God by the name of al-Llah. Since no idol was molded to represent that invisible God, they had begun worshiping other gods who were fashioned as idols, but remaining conscious of the One God of their ancestors.

Below is a partial comment from an editor of Islamic publication, condoning violence and justifying the acts of the hate-mongering extremists.

Even ISIS is legitimate response we can understand. Mass killing of innocent children in thousands cannot go unpunished. These are all natural consequences. Please see the root cause of these problems Muslims now facing. Americans are killing Muslims on daily basis and you do not expect that there will be no reactions from Muslims (The Other Press/Selangor).

And yet, Muslims are killing Muslims and non-Muslims are coming to their rescue for peace and sanity in the world? Americans and Europeans, French and Canadians, Arabs and non-Arabs, just to name a few, to end this spree of bloodbath and vengeance. Kill vengeance, not men, and peace will be gained!

A twenty first century Muslim student, candidly and practically, would neither read volumes upon volumes of Hadiths, nor would be inclined to explore the validity or absurdity of the words written, rewritten and rigged with repetitions. Most of the Hadiths as traditions of the Prophet are rigged with false statements, portraying the Prophet Muhammad as a harsh man, issuing edicts of intolerance, forbidding good things in life, subjecting women to unfair treatment and obedience to men, and promoting warfare. Though truthfully and historically, the Prophet Muhammad was the kindest, gentlest and the most tolerant of men, living Islam by the example of his life. Only a small fraction of traditions in Hadith portray the Prophet as a kind, loving, tolerant, and compassionate man. A Prophet promoting the virtues of peace, justice, and equality is allotted a very limited space in the chronicles of Hadith.

The time is ripe in this twenty first century to challenge the validity of Hadiths, to wade through the rivers of Traditions and to perform the ritual of purification, so that the scriptures are purged clean of all dross matter of fabrication. Salvaging only the noble character of the Prophet, which would fit in one small volume of Hadith, young Muslim students would get to know Islam as the religion of love, harmony, and reconciliation.

Paradoxically, it is quite critical that most Muslim writers writing about Sunnah have filled volumes upon volumes with insignificant details and not much about the essence of Islam as the religion of love, unity, and forgiveness. Even Fiqh-us-Sunnah has devoted a quarter of its pages talking about how the Prophet Muhammad urinated and cleaned his private parts, going as far as explaining bluntly and crudely how he washed his penis and how he prayed after relieving himself. The rest of the book reiterates which hand to use for what and which foot to lift first before entering or leaving the mosque. Manifold repetitions, contradictory restrictions concerning the ritual prayers, and a plethora of erroneous traditions are sure to overwhelm the twenty first century reader with disgust and confusion.

Since Muslims have distorted the message of the Prophet Muhammad so magnanimously, historians and theologians need to scrape clean the windows of the un-Islamic Sharia with its human interpretation, to have a glimpse of the Prophet's Sharia. This book is an attempt to wash off all the windows of walled literature, scrubbing them clean of the countless distortions and misconceptions, reflecting the original portrait of Islam as painted by the Prophet in synchronicity with his character as a loving, forgiving, compassionate Messenger of Peace, and universal equality.

No valid definition of Sharia exists and a potpourri of those which are being tossed around are countless, concocted by the clerics, historians, and theologians. Such definitions were written and rewritten by the so-called scholars several years after the death of the Prophet Muhammad with interpretations to suit their own ways of thinking and permit no room for the proof of validity, criticism, or discussion. The origin of Sharia, even the most orthodox of theologians would agree, is based on traditions gathered from the sayings and lifestyle of the Prophet and from the wealth of revelations compiled as the holy book of the Quran,.

Starting with the Sunna—the exemplary life of the Prophet Muhammad, if Muslims were to follow in his footsteps, there would be left not even a trace of cruelty, hatred, bigotry or violence in Islam. Hoping that reason, as the Prophet Muhammad claimed reason to be the most precious of God-given gifts, would tempt theologians to open a dialogue with a string of discussions in the very ether of cyberspace, if not in the arena of global syllogisms. The revelations were amongst many of the Prophet's God-given gifts which served him as his talisman of Divine Guidance since the inception of his message until his death. Against the weight of persecutions, he didn't leave Mecca until permission was granted to him by God in a revelation. Peaceful by nature, he desisted from fighting the Meccans until a revelation permitted him to engage in a battle against them with an injunction that only after all means of peace efforts were exhausted.

# Table of Contents

# Chapter 1 ~ Prophet's Sharia

*And we have not sent thee but as a mercy to the nations.* (Quran 21:107)

The Prophet's Sharia, before it was hijacked by the scholars turned bigots and zealots, was in all its purity the law of love, peace and harmony. He lived this law by the example of his life as a loving, compassionate and forgiving man of words and deeds. He interpreted revelations in such a profound manner so as to polish the precepts of Islam with the gold of love, tolerance and harmony. As it is stated in this revelation below.

*He it is who hath revealed unto thee Muhammad the Scripture wherein are clear revelations. They are the substance of the Book—and others which are allegorical. But those in whose hearts is doubt pursue, forsooth, that which is allegorical, seeking to cause dissention by seeking to explain it. None knoweth its explanation save Allah. And those who are of sound instruction say: we believe therein, the whole is from our Lord, but only men of understanding really heed.* (Quran 3:7)

The Prophet had to deal with the zeal of his followers at the very inception of Islam. One day the Prophet was sitting in the mosque in Medina when Abdullah, the son of Abdallah ibn Ubbay, came suddenly to share the news of his father's death and of his last request before he died that the Prophet give his shirt as a burial shroud and to come and pray at his funeral. The Prophet got to his feet to fulfil the last wishes of Abdallah ibn Ubbay, but his followers started protesting, knowing the deceased to be marked as a hypocrite during his lifetime. Saying, how could he, the Prophet, agree to grant the last requests of Abdullah's father against the weight of the recent revelation?

*Ask forgiveness for them O Muhammad or ask not forgiveness for them. Though thou ask forgiveness for them seventy times, Allah will not forgive them. That is because they disbelieved in Allah and His Messenger, and Allah guideth not wrongdoing folk.* (Quran 9:80)

The Prophet turned to his heels, commenting over his shoulders, "I have to pray more than seventy times then, don't I?"

One revelation which was dear to his heart:

*Keep to forgiveness O Muhammad and enjoin kindness, and turn away from the ignorant.* (Quran 7:199)

The Prophet's forgiveness was unconditional and his love boundless. After the conquest of Mecca he forgave everyone, even Hind the wife of Abu Sofyan who had chewed on the heart of his slain uncle Hamza. When Abu Sofyan wished to accept Islam, the Prophet said that if he was willing to accept it for fear that he would be punished if he did not, then he should not be willing. For no punishment was forthcoming and that he should wait 'til he could accept it without fear and with all his heart.

The Prophet's own love extended to all God's creatures. Once during a sermon, a cat took the liberty of sitting over the edge of his robe and he wouldn't get up lest he disturb the cat. At the time of his final pilgrimage to Mecca, he noticed a bitch on the road with a litter of pups and commanded his men to change their route so as not to frighten the young pups.

He abhorred war and succumbed to its dictates only as a last resort after all efforts at peace were exhausted. The Peace Treaty which the Prophet signed under the Lote Tree lent so much advantage to the pagans that his own followers were angry and resentful. But he stayed firm, guided by his wisdom and by the wealth of the revelations. His favorite expression, "No person has drunk a better draught than that of anger which he has swallowed for God's sake."

*And if they incline to peace, incline thou also to it, and trust in Allah. Lo, He is the Hearer, the Knower.* (Quran 8:61)

Again and again the Prophet had to guide even his loved ones on the path to compassion and tolerance.

Once Omar dragged a man away from the precincts of the mosque when he saw him urinating by the wall. Later, Omar told the Prophet that the man had defiled the mosque so he had thrown him out. The Prophet reprimanded Omar, saying that since he treated the man roughly he must find him and apologize, adding that a pail of water would have purified the spot.

During the lifetime of the Prophet, dogs used to urinate and pass through the mosque, and no water was sprinkled on it. Al Bukhari [1:174(B)-O.B]

A Bedouin stood up and started making water in the mosque. The people caught him with the intention of throwing him out, but Prophet reprimanded them, saying, that a bucket of water over the place where he has urinated would be enough to clean the spot. Adding that you have been sent to make things easy and not to make them difficult. Al Bukhari [1:219-O.B

Living amidst the countless tides of zeal and intolerance, the Prophet was heard exclaiming, "By these pious fools my back hath been broken."

To the very end of his life the Prophet strove toward cultivating the seeds of love, peace and harmony.

He had forbidden the use of weapons before journeying from Medina to Mecca, he and his followers going there as pilgrims, not as warriors. As he and his cavalcade approached closer to Mecca, Saeed bin Udabah began brandishing his sword and exclaiming, "Today is the day of fighting."

The Prophet was quick to snatch the sword from him and hand it over to his son, Abu Qays. Reproof spilling down from his lips, "This is how you distort the message of the Prophet, O Saeed?"

*Lo who distort our revelations are not hid from us. It is he who is hurled into the fire better or he who cometh secure on the Day of Resurrection? Do what you will. Lo, He is seer of what you do.* (Quran 41:40)

After the conquest of Mecca, quite a few reprimands landed on Ali since he was the closest and the most beloved. The Prophet was talking to Othman ibn Talha when Ali snatched the keys of the Kaaba from him, saying, "These keys now belong to the Prophet of Islam."

"Ali, be kind and loving and return those keys to Othman." The Prophet Muhammad commanded sadly and swiftly. "Have I failed in my message of equal love and equal respect for all? He is not one of us who incites bigotry, or fights for bigotry or dies in its pursuit."

Another scene of discord ensued soon after when the Prophet's wives were urging Ali's sister Umm Hani not to seek protection for her husband Hudayfah who was an idolater. Ali was amongst them, threatening to kill his sister and her husband when the Prophet appeared on this scene of contention.

"I seek protection for my husband." Umm Hani flung her cloak over the shoulders of her husband and ran to the Prophet, and was received into his loving arms, sobbing uncontrollably.

"Whom you make safe, dear Umm Hani, him we make safe. Whom you protect, we protect." Prophet Muhammad turned to Ali. "Have you not been reprimanded for your zeal already?"

Another revelation close to Prophet's heart:

*O ye who believe! Be steadfast witness for Allah in equity, and let not the hatred of any people seduce you that you deal not justly. Deal justly that is nearer to your duty. Observe your duty to Allah. Lo, Allah is informed of what you do.* (Quran 5:8)

In a polygamous society when the Arab men had several wives and concubines, the Prophet Muhammad remained faithful to Khadija alone for twenty-four years of blissful marriage. After her death he contracted more marriages with women who were widows and needed protection, with the exception of only one, Aisha, who was a virgin.

The description of the Prophet's character by Aisha in one of the Hadiths: He laughed a lot and never held a grudge against anyone.

After the conquest of Mecca he said, *Have no fear this day! May Allah forgive you and He is the most merciful of those who show mercy.* (Quran 12:92)

No one was coerced into becoming a Muslim, though many Meccans came out of their own free will to accept Islam.

Bilal—Islam's first Muezzin quoting Prophet Muhammad in one of the Hadiths says, "If a Muslim forces a conversion, he doesn't risk hell, he is certain of hell."

During the lifetime of the Prophet Muhammad wealthy Meccans owned slaves and treated them unfairly. The Prophet Muhammad even before he received any revelation was a staunch opponent of this evil practice. After he started preaching Islam, he freed his slave Zaid given to him by his first wife Khadija and adopted him as his son. His companions followed suit and his closest of friends, Abu Bakr purchased several slaves from the rich Meccans to grant them freedom. One most prominent amongst them was an Ethiopian slave by the name of Bilal who became the first muezzin of Islam. Slowly and gradually, the Prophet Muhammad received revelations dear to his heart which encouraged the emancipation of slaves and promoted the abolition of slavery.

*It is not righteousness that ye turn your face to the East and the West, but righteous is he who believeth in Allah and the Last Day and the angels and the Scripture and the Prophets and giveth his wealth for love of Him, to kinsfolk and to orphans and the needy and the wayfarer and to those who ask and To* Set Slaves Free, *and observeth proper worship and payeth the poor due. And those who keep their treaty when they make one, and patient in tribulation and adversity and time of stress. Such are they who are sincere. Such are God-fearing.* (Quran 2:177)

*We verily have created man into toil and struggle. Thinketh he that none have power over him. And he saith: I have destroyed vast wealth. Thinketh he that none beholdeth him. Did We not assign unto him two eyes and a tongue and two lips? And guide him to the parting of the mountain ways. But he hath not attempted the Ascent. Ah, what will convey to thee what the Ascent is? It is to* Free a Slave. (Quran 90:4-13)

*It is not for a believer to kill a believer unless it is by mistake. He who hath killed a believer by mistake must Set Free a Believing Slave and pay the blood money to the family of the slain, unless they remit it as a charity. If he the victim be of people hostile unto you and he is a believer, then the penance is to Set Free a Believing Slave. And if he cometh of a folk between whom and you is a covenant, then the blood money must be paid unto his folk and also a Believing Slave Must be Set Free. And whoso hath not the wherewithal must fast two consecutive months. A penance from Allah. Allah is Knower, Wise.* (Quran 4:92)

*Allah will not take you to task for that is unintentional in your oaths, but He will take you to task for the oaths ye swear in earnest. The expiation thereof is the feeding of the ten of the needy with the average of that wherewith ye feed your own folk, or the clothing of the, or the* Liberation of a Slave, *and for him who findeth not the wherewithal to do so, then a three day fast. This is the expiation of your oaths when you have sworn and keep your oaths. Thus Allah expoundeth unto you His revelations in order that ye may give thanks.* (Quran 5:89)

*And let those who cannot find a match keep chaste till Allah give them independence by His grace. And such of your* Slaves *as seek a writing of Emancipation, write it for them if ye are aware of aught of good in them, and* *bestow upon them of the wealth of Allah which He hath bestowed upon you. Force not your <u>Slave-Girls</u> to Whoredom that ye may seek enjoyment of the life of the world, if they would preserve their chastity.* (Quran 24:33)

*And in no wise covet those things in which Allah has bestowed his gifts more freely on some of you than others. To men is allotted what they earn, and to women is allotted what they earn.* (Quran 4: 32)

## Adultery

Muslims have made a mockery of their own religion by presenting Islam as the most hateful and intolerant of all religions without even a trace of love or compassion. Many women from Iran to Syria to Pakistan, to Afghanistan, who were stoned to death for adultery, were the victims of the savages, blackening the name of Islam with lies and distortion. Quran doesn't sanction murder of the adulterer or the adulteress, or stoning to death for women. Quranic verses are suggestive of punishment, but lean more toward forgiveness. If in one verse a punishment is ascribed, the next one talks about mercy and forgiveness.

"Let the man who has not sinned, throw the first stone at the Jewish adulteress." These words of Christ still appeal to the sea of corruption in the hearts of men with the intention of purifying it with the flood of love, compassion and understanding. And yet no Muslim woman was stoned to death during the life of the Prophet Muhammad.

*And come not near unto adultery. Lo, it is an abomination and an evil way.* (Quran 17: 32)

*And for those of your women who are guilty of lewdness, call on witness four of you against them. And if they testify to the truth of the allegation, then confine them to the houses until death take them or until Allah appoint for them a way through new legislation.* (Quran 4:15)

*And as for two of you who are guilty thereof, punish them both. And if they repent and improve, then let them be. Lo, Allah is Relenting, Merciful.* (Quran 4:17)

"Prophet said, if you accuse your wife of adultery, bring four witnesses." Al Bukhari [6:269-O.B]

*And as for two of you who are guilty thereof, punish them both. And if they repent, let them be. Allah is relenting, merciful.* (Quran 4:16) And yet again, no Muslim woman was stoned to death during the life of the Prophet Muhammad even after the revelation below which doesn't excuse the adulterer, since both are to be punished equally. *The adulterer and the adulteress, scourge ye each with hundred stripes.* (Quran 24:2)

Where are the nameless, faceless adulterers when women are being scourged brutally by the pious, ignorant men, blinded by the shafts of their own cruelty, hypocrisy and malfeasance? How can the All Merciful, Infinitely Compassionate Allah sanction murder when killing is forbidden in Islam? And yet this one controversial verse below has the weight of gold for the extremists who would rather punish than forgive.

*The adulterer and the adulteress, scourge ye each one of them with a hundred stripes. And let not the pity for the twain withhold you from obedience to Allah, if ye believe in Allah and the Last Day. And let a party of believers witness their punishment.* (Quran 24:2)

Punishment for both male and female is suggested in this verse, but extremists use only one verse and neglect the other to fulfill their need for cruelty. The totality comes to life in forgiveness.

*As for the woman and the man, guilty of fornication, flog each of them with one hundred lashes. Let not compassion move you away in their case from carrying out God's law. Unless they repent and amend themselves, then God is Forgiving, Most Merciful.* (Quran 24:2, 5)

*And those who accuse chaste women and fail to produce four witnesses, flog them with eighty lashes and accept not their testimony ever after, for they are transgressors. Except for those who repent and reform themselves, then God is Forgiving, Most Merciful.* (Quran 42:4)

Apostasy, too, which is viewed as a crime deserving harsh punishments, is the perception of the extremists, not consistent with the Quranic injunctions.

*They question thee O Muhammad with regard to warfare in the Sacred Month. Say: Warfare therein is great transgression, but to turn men from the way of Allah and to disbelieve in Him and in the Inviolable place of Worship, and to expel people thence is greater with Allah, for persecution is greater than killing. And they will not cease from fighting against you till they have made you renegades from your religion, if they can. And whoso becometh a renegade and dieth in his disbelief, such are they whose works have fallen both in the world and the Hereafter.* (Quran 2: 217)

*O ye who believe! Whoso of you becometh a renegade from his religion, know that in his stead Allah will bring a people whom He loveth and who love Him. Humble toward believers, stern toward disbelievers, striving in the way of Allah and fearing not the blame of any blamer. Such is the grace of Allah which He giveth unto whom He will. Allah is All-Knowing, All-Embracing.* (Quran 5: 54)

*Say: O my servants who have transgressed against your own selves, do not despair of Allah's Compassion. For Allah is often forgiving, infinitely merciful. Turn to your Sustainer and surrender to Him before the suffering comes upon you. After that you will not be helped. And before the penalty suddenly comes upon you, without your perceiving it. Follow the best which your Sustainer had revealed to you.* (Quran 39:53-55)

The Prophet Muhammad promoted the virtue of reason before judgment. Once a man from the tribe of Beni Fazarah came to the Prophet Muhammad, accusing his wife of adultery since she had given birth to a black child. The Prophet Muhammad asked him if he had any camels and the man replied in the affirmative. Then he enquired about the color of the camels and the man said, red. The Prophet Muhammad asked if there was a black amongst them and the man said, yes. Again, Prophet Muhammad asked, why is that so? The man replied, maybe due to the genealogical tendency. Your child, too, must have been born due to such a tendency, the Prophet Muhammad comforted him, enjoining him to treat his wife with trust and loving kindness.

## Jihad

The word Jihad does not mean holy war, it means struggle against evil. The Quran permits only defensive warfare. The Prophet Muhammad condemned war as one of the many evils and forbade the Muslims to initiate warfare. Telling them that when war is inevitable in case of self-defense, civilian deaths must be avoided, women and children must not be killed, no trees are to be cut down and no buildings to be burnt down.

## Fasting/Hajj

*War is a great transgression in the sacred month of Ramadan.* (Quran 2:217)

*And eat and drink until the white thread becometh distinct to you from the black thread of the dawn. These are the bounds set by God. Do not then offend against them. It is thus that God makes clear His messages unto mankind, so that they might remain conscious of Him.* (Quran 2:187)

*O ye who believe! Profane not Allah's monuments nor the sacred month nor the offerings nor the garlands, nor those repairing to the Sacred House, seeking the grace and pleasure of Allah. But when you have left the sacred territory, then go hunting (if you will) and let not your hatred of a folk who once stopped you going to the Inviolable Place of Worship seduce you to transgress, but help ye one another unto righteousness and pious duty. Help not one another unto sin and transgression, but keep your duty to Allah. Lo, Allah is severe in punishment.* (Quran 5: 2)

*The pilgrimage is in the well-known months, and whoever is minded to perform the pilgrimage therein, let him remember that there is to be no abuse nor lewdness nor angry conversation on the pilgrimage. And whatsoever good ye do Allah knoweth it. So make provisions for yourselves hereafter, for best provision is to ward off evil. Therefore keep your duty unto Me, O men of understanding.* (Quran 2: 197)

*Lo, the mountains As-Safa and Al-Marwah are among the indications of Allah. It is therefore no sin for him who is on a pilgrimage to the House of God or visiteth it, to go around them as the pagan custom is. And he who doeth good of his own accord, for him, lo, Allah is Aware, Responsive.* (Quran 2: 158)

*O ye who believe, fasting is prescribed for you, even as it was prescribed for those before you, that ye may ward off evil.* (Quran 2: 183)

When the Prophet Muhammad received his first revelation, some of the Arabs were convinced that Allah, the High God of their pantheon, was identical with the God of the Jews and the Christians. Christian Arabs often made pilgrimage to Kaaba, commonly regarded as Allah's shrine in Mecca, alongside the pagans. One of the first things that the Prophet asked his followers to do was to pray facing Jerusalem, the city of the Jews and the Christians, whose God they were now going to worship. No Jews or Christians were required, or even invited to join the new Arab religion unless they particularly wished to do so, because they had received solid revelations of their own. In the Quran God told the Muslims that they must treat the People of the Book with respect and courtesy. (Karen Armstrong).

Eat and drink and do not be misled by the ascending white light. Eat and drink until the redness of dawn appears. During fasting a person should not behave foolishly or impudently. Or if somebody fights with him or abuses him, he should just say to him twice, I am observing fast. Prophet Muhammad Al Bukhari [3:118-O.B]

Aisha narrated, I used to scent Allah's Messenger when he wanted to assume Ihram and also on finishing Ihram before the Tawaf around Kaaba.

 The pilgrims who did not have Badana and had not garlanded them, were permitted to have sexual relations with their wives, using perfume and wearing ordinary clothes. Then they could assume Ihram if they wanted to perform Hajj. Al Bukhari [2:617-O.B]

Omar narrated, there is no reason for us to do Tawaf except that we wanted to show off before the pagans, and now Allah has destroyed them. But Prophet did Tawaf and we do not want to leave it. Omar narrated that he waited for Al-Hajjaj before proceeding toward Arafat during the pilgrimage till he was done bathing. Al Bukhari [2:722-O.B]

Jabir said that a person in a state of ihram may take a bath and wash his grab. Fiqh-us-Sunnah

Prophet in a state of Ihram used to wash his head, rubbing with his hands from back to front and from front to back. Al Bukhari [3:66-O.B]

Aisha related that Messenger of Allah permitted women to wear shoes while in a state of ihram. Fiqh-us-Sunnah

The Prophet said, I have made Al-Medina a sanctuary between its two mountains. Al Bukhari [3:93-O.B]

The Prophet said, whoever does not give up lying speech and acting on those lies and evil actions, Allah is not in need of his leaving his food and drink. Allah will not accept his fast. Al Bukhari [3:127-O.B]

The Prophet said, during Ramadan eat and drink until the white thread of dawn appears to you distinct from the black thread of the night. Al Bukhari [3:140-O.B]

Aisha narrated, the Prophet used to kiss and embrace his wives while he was observing fast and he had more power to control his desires than any of you. Al Bukhari [3:149-O.B]

The Prophet said, it is not righteousness to observe fast on a journey. Al Bukhari [3:167-O.B]

The Prophet said, if meat is brought to you and you are not sure that the name of Allah is not mentioned on it before slaughtering, mention the name of Allah and eat it. Al Bukhari [3:273-O.B]

The Prophet said a man in a state of ihram should not wear a shirt, a turban, trousers or head-cloak or a garment scented with saffron or Wars (a kind of perfume). And if he has no slippers he can wear leather socks, but the socks should be cut short so as the make the ankles bare. Al Bukhari [1:136-O.B]

If a woman's clothes are spoiled due to menses, she should rub it with water till it is clean, then she can offer prayer wearing the same clothes. Al Bukhari [1:227-O.B]

Aisha said, the Prophet used to lean on my lap and recite Quran while I was in menses. Al Bukhari [1:296-O.B]

Umm Salma narrated the Prophet used to kiss me while he was observing fast. Al Bukhari [1:319-O.B]

Maymuna narrated that during her menses she didn't offer prayers, but used to sit beside the mosque of the Prophet. He used to offer prayer on his sheet and in prostration some of his clothes used to touch me. Al Bukhari [1:329-O.B]

## Traditions of Prophet

The Prophet said, the example of one who glorifies (Dhikr) Allah in comparison to the one who does not glorify Allah is that of a living creature compared to a dead one. Al Bukhari [8:416-O.B] The Prophet said, a Muslim is the one who avoids harming Muslims with his hands and tongue. And an emigrant is the one who abandons all that Allah has forbidden. Al Bukhari [1:9-O.B] The Prophet said, religion is very easy and whoever overburdens himself in his religion will not be able to continue in that way. So you should not be extremists, but try to be near to perfection and receive the good tidings that you will be rewarded and gain strength by offering prayers in the mornings, afternoons and during the last hours of the nights. Al Bukhari [1:38-O.B]

The Prophet said, both legal and illegal things are evident, but in between them there are doubtful things, and most of the people have no knowledge about them. So whoever saves himself from these doubtful things he saves his religion and his honor. And whoever indulges in these doubtful things is like a shepherd who grazes his animals near the private pasture of someone else, and at any moment he is liable to get in it. Beware there is a piece of flesh in the body, if it becomes good the whole body becomes good, but if it gets spoilt the whole body gets spoilt and that is the heart. Al Bukhari [1:49-O.B]

The Prophet said, religious knowledge will be taken away by the death of religious scholars. Ignorance in religion and trials and afflictions will increase by killing of each other. Al Bukhari [1:85-O.B]

The Prophet said, Allah does not take away the knowledge by taking it away from the hearts of the people, but takes it away by the death of the religious learned men till when none of the religious learned men remains. People will take as their leaders ignorant persons who when consulted will give their verdict without knowledge. So they will go astray and will lead the people astray. Al Bukhari [1:100-O.B]

The Prophet said, do not become infidels after me by cutting the throats of one another. Al Bukhari [1:122-O.B]

The men used to offer prayer with the Prophet with their Izar tied around their necks as boys used to do, therefore the Prophet told the women not to raise their heads from prostration till the men sat down straight while praying. Al Bukhari [1:358-OB]

Anas related that at times the Prophet used to offer prayers with his shoes on. Al Bukhari [1:383-O.B]

The Prophet ordered a horse race. Trained horses were to run from Al-Hafya to Thanlyat-ul-Wadi. Untrained horses were to run from Al-Thaniya to the mosque of Bani Zuraiq. Al Bukhari [1:412-O.B]

From now onwards this community of the Ansar will decrease and other people will increase. So anybody who becomes a ruler of the followers of Muhammad and had the power to harm or benefit people, then he should accept the good from the benevolent amongst the Ansar and overlook the faults of their wrongdoers. Al Bukhari [2:49-O.B]

A man was inflicted with wounds and he committed suicide. So Allah said, My slave has caused death on himself hurriedly, so I forbid paradise for him. Al Bukhari [2:445-OB]

The writers of Hadith, firm believers in inclusion, not exclusion, were writing what they heard, not necessarily true, and this comment from the Prophet is disputed by scholars. Some say it is not in consonant with the Prophet's character and others believe it to be authentic.

In order to live Islam by the example of Prophet's life, Muslims need to read authentic Hadiths carefully, gleaning truth as to how Prophet Muhammad wanted Muslims to lead a harmonious life. His sayings below are testament to the fact of living Islam virtuously.

**Prophet Muhammad's sayings from Hadiths:**

The Islam of heart is its purity, and the Islam of tongue withholding it from fruitless words. A man cannot be a Muslim until his heart and tongue are so.

Shall I inform you of a better act than alms, prayers and fasting? Making peace between one another. Enmity and malice tear up the heavenly rewards by the roots.

If you can keep your heart from morning till night and from night till morning free from malice toward anyone, you are following my path and he who loveth my path verily loveth me. God is one and liketh unity.

Do you love your creator? Love your fellow beings first.

It can happen that a man will seem to have the behavior of the elect while instead he would be amongst the damned. It can happen that man will seem to be among the damned while instead he will be one of the elect. Conscience: if you derive pleasure from the good which you perform, and be grieved for the evil which you have committed, you are a true believer. The best of the God's servants are those who, when seen, remind of God, and the worst of God's servants are those who carry tales about, to do mischief and separate friends, and seek for the defects of the good. Humility and courtesy are acts of piety. Abuse nobody, and if a man abuse you and lay open a vice which he knows in you, then do not disclose the one which you know in him. Meekness and modesty are two branches of faith, and vain talking and embellishing are two branches of hypocrisy.

He is of the most perfect Muslims, whose disposition is most liked by his family. To do unto all men as you would wish to have done unto you, and to reject for others what you would reject for yourself. Adore God as if you saw Him, for if you see Him not, He sees you. Feed the hungry and visit the sick, and free the captive, if he be unjustly confined. Assist any person oppressed, whether Muslim or non-Muslim. The proof of a Muslim's sincerity is that he pays no heed to what is not his business. The faithful are those who perform their trust and fail not in their word, and keep their pledge. That person is not one of us who invites others to aid him in oppression, and he is not one of us who fights for his tribe in injustice, and he is not one of us who dies in assisting his tribe in tyranny.

Do not say, that if people do good to us, we will do good to them, and if people oppress us, we will oppress them; but determine, that if people do you good, you will do good to them, and if they oppress you, you will not oppress them. There is a polish for everything that takes away rust, and the polish for the heart is the remembrance of God. Verily those who are patient in adversity and forgive wrongs are the doers of excellence. That person is nearest to God, who pardons, when he has in his power to injure who would have injured him.

God is gentle and loves gentleness. God says: The person I hold as a beloved, I am his hearing by which he hears, and I am his sight by which he sees, and I am his hands by which he holds, and I am his feet by which he walks. God is One and likes unity; God said: I was a hidden treasure. I would fain be known. So I created Man. God is not merciful to him who is not so to mankind.

God says: verily my compassion overcomes my wrath. If you put your whole trust in God, as you aught, He most certainly will give you sustenance, as He does the birds, they come out hungry in the morning, but return full to their nests. O My servants who have oppressed your own souls by sinning, despair not of the Mercy of God (when asked what about the unbelievers) know that him also God forgives, if he repents. If the unbeliever knew of the extent of the Lord's mercy, even he would not despair of Paradise. Islam is purity of speech and charity.

Excellent actions are: to gladden the heart of a human being, to feed the hungry, to help the afflicted, to lighten the sorrow of the sorrowful, and to remove the wrongs of the injured. Whoever is kind to His creatures, God is kind to him, therefore be kind to everyone on earth, whether good or bad.

He dies not who gives life to learning. An hour's contemplation is better than a year's adoration; go in quest of knowledge even unto China. Seek knowledge from cradle to grave. What weakens the foundations of Islam: the errors of the learned destroy it, the disputations of the hypocrites, and the orders of the kings who have lost the road. To spend more time in learning is better than spending more time in praying. It is better to teach knowledge one hour in the night than to pray the whole night. The pursuit of knowledge is a divine commandment for every Muslim, male or female. God hath treasuries beneath the Throne, the keys whereof are the tongues of poets; he who knows his own self knows God. Acquire knowledge. It enables its possessor to distinguish from right and wrong; it lights the way to Heaven; it is our friend in the desert; our society in solitude; our companion when friendless; it guides us to happiness; it sustains us in misery; it is an ornament amongst friends and an armor against enemies. To the light I have attained and in light I live. O Lord, grant me the love of Thee, grant that I love those who love Thee, grant that I may do the deeds that win Thy love, make Thy love dearer to me than self, wealth or family.

O Lord, I make my complaint unto Thee, of my feebleness, the vanity of my efforts. I am insignificant in the sight of men, O Thou Most Merciful. Lord of the weak, Thou art my Lord. Forsake me not. Leave me not a prey to strangers, nor to mine enemies. If Thou art not displeased, I am safe. I seek refuge in the Light of Thy Countenance, by which all darkness is dispelled, and peace cometh in the Here and Hereafter. Solve Thou my difficulties as it pleaseth Thee. There is no power, no strength, save in Thee. This was Prophet's prayer when he was persecuted and wounded at Taif. Prayer is the annihilation of ego and union with the Divine, which lifts one's soul higher and higher in its journey toward the Beloved.

He whom prayer preventeth not from evil and wrongdoing, increaseth in naught save in remoteness from the Lord. God is beauty and delights in the beautiful, but pride is holding man in contempt. They will enter the garden of Bliss who have true, pure and merciful heart. God has not created anything better than Reason, or anything more perfect, or more beautiful than Reason; the benefits which God gives are on its account; and understanding is by it, and God's wrath is caused by disregard of it.

He is perfect who does good to his relatives when they do not do good to him. Much silence and a good disposition, there are no two works better than those.

No man is true in the truest sense of the word but he who is true in word, in deed, and in thought. It is not worthy of a speaker of truth to curse people. He is not of me who, when he speaks, speaks falsely; who, when he promises, breaks his promise; and who, when trust is reposed in him, fails in his trust. To die before dying, to die to the darkness within, and to live in the Light of God.

The ink of a scholar is more holy than the blood of a martyr. Say unto the people of the Scripture: dispute ye with us concerning Allah when He is our Lord and your Lord? Ours are our works and yours your works. The Prophet said that on the day of resurrection, God will manifest Himself to the creatures in the forms that they themselves refuted, announcing I am your Lord. In the face of this unfamiliar apparition, they will seek refuge in their own representation of God. Then God will appear in that representation, and then they will believe that indeed it is Him.

Mughira says: I sent a message to a woman asking for her hand. The Prophet said to me: Have a look at her before marrying, for that will enhance love and mutual regard between you. God sent to the world since its creation two hundred thousand prophets, twenty-five of them are referred in the Quran. The greatest of those are Adam, Noah, Abraham, Moses, Jesus and Muhammad. Prophets are to be regarded as free from sin, the most sinless of all being Jesus. Muhammad speaks of him as the Word of God, the Spirit of God, born of the Virgin Mary, and Worker of Miracles.

Sharia by the very nature of its vagueness and conflicting views is valid if its aim is to protect and invalid if it seeks to harm.

# Chapter 2 ~ Women in the Quran and Sunnah

What is Sharia? Simply, it is the law of Islam, also characterized as Jurist's Law. What is the goal of Sharia? If its goal is to enforce hatred, cruelty, injustice and intolerance, based on interpretations from the Quranic revelations and Traditions of the Prophet, then it is in sore need of amendment. However, there is no need of amendment if Sharia could be rescued from the jungle of its interpretations, so gnarled and distorted, and then presented in the purity of its essence as the law of peace, justice and equality. The authors of zeal have scraped out a handful of verses from the Quran with their own interpretations to suit their need for murder, misogyny and malfeasance, sidelining ninety-nine percent of the verses, brimming with love, peace, mercy and tolerance. The same is true with the Traditions of the Prophet, depicting him as a harsh, hateful, warring man of strict disposition and ignoring ninety-nine percent of his sayings which reveal his noble character as a man of great virtues, loving, peaceful and compassionate. In fact, the Prophet Muhammad was a modern day activist in that age and time, liberating women from the shackles of injustice and inequality.

Independent of Sharia, many pre-Islamic traditions of the pagan Arabs such as honor killing are erroneously attributed to Islam. Even in the 21st Century, when a woman is brutally and wrongfully stoned to death as the victim of honor killing, the Muslims piously admit that this has been going on for centuries, but this doesn't absolve them form the sin of letting this heinous crime breed and multiply. There is no justification for continuing to do so under the banner of Islam and in this case each Muslim male stands guilty of moral neglect by dishonoring their women publicly and shamelessly. Aside from a few controversial verses in the Quran exposed to misinterpretations from the zealots of Islam to meet the needs of their control to exploit and tyrannize, the majority of verses are closed to misinterpretation by the very virtue of their purity and simplicity. Since the message of love, peace and unity is the theme of such verses, they are foremost part of

Sharia and are presented below for the benefit of Muslim men and women. The controversial verses would be at the end of this chapter with an attempt at correct interpretation.

*O mankind! Lo, We have created you male and female, and have made you nations and tribes that ye may know one another. Lo, the noblest of you in the sight of Allah is the best in conduct. Lo, Allah is Knower, Aware.* (Quran 49:13)

*Women shall have the same rights over men as men have over them.* (Quran 2:228)

*And the women have rights similar to those of men in equity. I God will allow not the work of any worker from among you, male or female, to be lost.* (Quran 3:196)

*And whoso doeth good works, whether male or female, and he or she is a believer, such will enter Paradise and they will not be wronged the dint in a date-stone.* (Quran 4:124)

*Whoso doeth right, whether male or female, and is a believer, all such will enter the Garden, where they will be nourished without stint.* (Quran 40:40)

*Allah promiseth to the believers, men and women, Gardens underneath which rivers flow, wherein they will abide—blessed dwellings in the Garden of Eden. And greater far acceptance from Allah. That is the supreme triumph.* (Quran 9:72)

*And the believers, men and women, are protecting friends one of another, they enjoin the right and forbid the wrong, and they establish worship and they pay the poor due, and they obey Allah and His messenger. As for those, Allah will have mercy on them. Lo, Allah is Mighty, Wise.* (Quran 9:71)

*Beautified for mankind is love of the joys that come from women and offspring, and stored-up heaps of gold and silver, and horses and cattle and land. That is comfort of the life of the world. Allah, with Him is a more excellent abode.* (Quran 3:14)

*And of His signs is this: He created for you helpmates from yourselves that ye might find rest in them, and He ordained between you love and mercy. Lo, herein indeed are portents for folk who reflect.* (Quran 30: 21)

*Thou canst defer whom thou wilt of them and receive unto thee whom thou wilt, and whomsoever thou desirest of those whom thou has set aside temporarily, it is no sin for thee to receive her again, that is better, that they may be comforted and not grieve, and may all be pleased with what thou givest them. Allah knoweth what is in your hearts O men and Allah is Clement, Forgiving.* (Quran 33: 51)

*And give women that you marry their dower as a free gift.* (Quran 4:4)

*This day no soul is wronged in aught, nor are ye required aught save what ye used to do.* (Quran 36: 53)

*Let those who merit paradise this day are happily employed.* (Quran 36: 54)

*They and their wives, in pleasant shade, on thrones reclining.* (Quran 36: 55)

*Theirs the fruit of their good deeds and theirs all that they ask.* (Quran 36: 56)

*The word from Merciful Lord for them is: Peace.* (Quran 36: 57)

*Enter the Garden, ye and your wives, to be made glad.* (Quran 43: 70)

*Therein are brought round for them trays of gold and goblets, and therein is all that souls desire and eyes find sweet. And ye are immortal therein.* (Quran 43: 71)

*This is the Garden which ye are made to inherit because of what ye used to do.* (Quran 43: 72)

*Therein for you is fruit in plenty whence to eat.* (Quran 43: 73)

*Whoso doeth which is right, and believes whether male or female, him or her We will quicken to happy life.* (Quran 16: 97)

Prophet said, if your women ask permission to go to the mosque at night, allow them. Al Bukhari [1:824-O.B]

A woman who is adult and of sound mind may be married by virtue of her own consent although the contract may not have been made or acceded by her guardians, and this whether she be a virgin or otherwise. Shafi/Hadith

When a married couple is known to have cohabited for twenty years and then the wife claims that she had not been supported by her husband, the claim must be granted a hearing not withstanding its apparent incredulity. The husband will be required to provide necessary evidence and the mere fact of cohabitation is not enough to absolve him of the claim. Al Shafi

The husband is required to respect the individuality of his non-Muslim wife, he is therefore not allowed to press her into embracing Islam. Mohammad Hashim Kamali

*There shall be no compulsion in religion.* (Quran 2:256)

This verse above proclaims religious freedom and pluralism.

*If God had willed, everyone on the face of the earth would have been believers. Ask you then compelling the people to become believers?* (Quran 10:99)

*Let whosoever wills, believe, and whosoever wills, disbelieve.* (Quran 18:29)

*And you are not to compel people, so remind by the means of Quran those who take heed.* (Quran 50:45)

*Say to the unbelievers, unto you your religion, and unto me, my religion.* (Quran 109:6)

## Prophet Muhammad's Sayings

God enjoins you to treat women well, for they are your aunts, wives, mothers and daughters.

The rights of the women are sacred, see that women are maintained in the rights assigned to them.

Only a man of noble character can honor women and only a man of base intention will dishonor women.

The most perfect man of religion who excels in character is the one who gives best treatment to his womenfolk.

Women are the other half of men.

Fear God in respect of women.

Paradise lies under the feet of mother.

One who brings up three daughters, provides them with good education and arranges their marriages and treats them with fairness, deserves to be ushered into Paradise. Men and women are members of one another and must live on a footing of equity and kindness and practice equality.

A Muslim must not hate his wife, and if he be displeased with one bad quality in her, then let him be pleased with another which is good. What you must never do is to raise your hands against your wife. Treat each woman with respect and kindness.

### Women Scholars and Healers:

Many Muslim women during the lifetime of the Prophet Muhammad learned to read and write and to study and practice medicine. One of them was a woman by the name of Rufaidah. She was proficient in reading and writing and had studied the science of healing. She became the tutor of the Prophet Muhammad's wife Hafsa to teach her reading and writing. One day the Prophet Muhammad requested her to teach Hafsah the science of healing, especially, the cure for skin rash which was becoming common in Medina. Rufaidah also served as a nurse to the Medinese community and when the Prophet Muhammad pitched a tent for her in the courtyard of the mosque, it became her private hospital to treat all sorts of ailments. Besides being healers and scholars, Muslim women accompanied men on the battlefield, some serving in defense and others nursing the wounded. There were fourteen women in the battle of Uhud, bringing food, water and medicine to the soldiers. Amongst them was the Prophet Muhammad's own daughter, Fatima. The Prophet Muhammad made women integral to his plan for Muslim education and learning when he proclaimed: Acquisition of knowledge is obligatory for every Muslim, male and female.

*The Prophet fixed one day a week to teach women about religion. Once during the lesson he said that a woman whose two or three children die during her lifetime would be shielded from hellfire.* Al Bukhari [1:101-O.B]

## Prophet Muhammad's Injunctions

When you speak, speak the truth. Commit not rape; be chaste; have no impure desires; withhold your hands from striking, and from taking that which is bad and unlawful.

The best of God's servants are those who, when seen, remind of God; and the worst of God's servants are those who carry tales about, to do mischief and separate friends, and seek for the defects of the good.

What a Muslim must never do is to raise his hand against woman. Treat each woman with respect and kindness.

The greatest crimes are: to tell lies, to assault women, to murder your own species, to commit suicide.

Fear Allah regarding women. Verily you have married them with the trust of Allah, and made their bodies lawful with the word of Allah. You have got rights over them and they have got rights over you in respect of their food and clothing according to your means.

> May I inform you of the people of hellfire? They are all those violent, arrogant and stubborn people—oppressor of women. Prophet Muhammad/Al Bukhari [6:440-O.B]
>
> He who wrongs a Jew or a Christian, will have me as his accuser. Prophet Muhammad [Hadith 16]
>
> Non-combatants were not to be killed in battle, there being a prohibition against the killing of women and children.
>
> Pierre Crabites, an American judge in the Cairo mixed tribunals, after a long experience of Muslim law as administered in Egyptian capital said: Prophet Muhammad was the greatest champion of women's rights in view of what the Prophet said when women were treated as chattels in Arabia. Quoting Prophet: A woman must not be a despised creature to be ashamed of or to be ill-treated any more, but a person to love and cherish and respect, at her feet are the gates of paradise. (Sir Abdullah Suhrawardy).
>
> Omar used to say to the Prophet, let your wives be veiled, but Allah's Messenger did not do so. Al Bukhari [1:148-O.B]
>
> Ibn Umar reported: He heard the Messenger of Allah forbidding women in a state of ihram wearing gloves and veil and garments dyed with wars and saying that they might wear besides this what they liked of garments colored with safflower or made of silk or wool, or ornaments or trousers or shirt. Al-Bukhari (AD 11:29)
>
> During the lifetime of Prophet, men and women used to perform ablution together. Al Bukhari [1:45-O.B]
>
> Hijab and veiling is not Islamic, though many believe it to be so, including Muslim men and Muslim women who question not the veracity of such customs imposed by the so-called men of learning since centuries. Such customs have become solid beliefs, repeated so often by so many with such passion and persistency that they have assumed the aura of truth. Yet it is

possible to shatter this false aura of truth by chiseling away layers upon layers of lies where the purity of expression still breathes love and radiance within the pages of the Quran and the Hadith. There is not a single verse in the Quran with any injunction of veil or hijab. Below are verses from the Quran prone to misinterpretation by the arbiters of Islam, though a couple of those cited here neglected by Muslims are for men to be modest.

*Tell the believing men to lower their gaze and be modest. This is purer for them. Lo! Allah is aware of what they do.* (Quran 24:30) *And men who guard their modesty and women who guard their modesty, and men who remember Allah and women who remember-- Allah hath prepared for them forgiveness and a vast reward.* (Quran 33:35)

*And tell the believing women to lower their gaze and be modest, and to display their adornments only that which is apparent, and to draw their scarves over their bosoms.* (Quran 24:31)

This verse above was revealed in response to pagan women going around Kaaba, wearing low-neck dresses with their bosoms revealed.

*O ye who believe! Enter not the dwellings of the Prophet for a meal without waiting for the proper time, unless permission is granted you. But if you are invited, enter, and when your meal is ended, then disperse. Lingering not for conversation. Lo, that would cause annoyance to the Prophet and he would be shy of asking you to go, but Allah is not shy of the truth. And when ye ask of the wives of the Prophet anything, ask it from them from behind a curtain.* (Quran 33:53)

This verse above was revealed after the Prophet's marriage with Zainab. The wedding guests lingered over the feast and didn't leave until it was very late in the night.

The wearing of a veil was pre-Islamic custom observed by the women of the Sasanian society. The segregation of the sexes was also pre-Islamic, practiced in the regions of the Middle East and the Mediterranean. No evidence of veiling is in the Quran or Sunnah. During the lifetime of the Prophet, Muslim women participated in the public life and didn't wear hijab. The pagan women, as well as women from the Judeo-Christian background, wore veil and hijab as a mark of wealth, status and distinction. To instill the virtue of equality amongst Muslims the Prophet Muhammad forbade the Muslim women to wear veils. The pearls of Hadith below attest to this fact. (Abu Dawud 11:29) The veil was worn in Arabia as a mark of rank: and it was therefore disallowed, as pilgrimage required obliteration of all differences of rank. Forbidding a veil in a pilgrimage is a further conclusive proof that Holy Quran did not enjoin the wearing of veil, as in that case the prohibition here stated would be a contradiction of the Holy Quran. Gloves are not allowed because like the veil they are a mark of rank. Ornaments are allowed because they are not a mark of rank, and are worn by even ordinary people and laboring classes

The Messenger of Allah forbade women pilgrims from wearing gloves, veils, and clothes dyed with saffron or wars (a sweet smelling plant that was used to dye clothes yellow). Besides these, they may wear anything else, any color, silk clothes, ornaments, trousers or shirt or shoes (Abu Dawud, Al Baihaqi and Al-Hakim).

Bukhari reported that Aisha put on a garment that was dyed with usfur while she was in a state of ihram and she said, "A woman must neither wear a veil to cover her face, nor clothes dyed with saffron or other fragrant dying material." Aisha is of the opinion that there is no harm for women pilgrims in wearing ornaments, black or rose-colored clothes and shoes.

Bukhari and Ahmad reported, "A pilgrim woman must neither cover her face, nor wear gloves."

A later verse just for the protection of the ladies of the Prophet's household is subject to misinterpretation.

*O Prophet, tell thy wives to draw their cloaks round them when they go abroad. That will be better so that they may be recognized and not annoyed. Allah is ever Forgiving, Merciful.* (Quran 33:59)

Even after this revelation, the women companions of the Prophet did not wear hijab as they knew that the Quranic directive was addressed only to the Prophet's wives. The Muslim women's participation in the life of the community during this time was dignified and social encounters took place at the initiative of the men and women, when the occasion arose. Mohammad Hashim Kamali

Below is an excerpt from the last sermon of the Prophet on the Mount of Mercy. This last sermon of the Prophet is epitome of Islam, a reminder to all Muslims how Islam should be lived by virtue of love, justice, empathy, harmony, tolerance, forgiveness. It is a mirror of right conduct—Sharia in its true essence, where hate, cruelty, prejudice, violence, enslavement are not admitted.

## From Last Sermon on the Mount

You have rights over your wives, and your wives have rights over you. Treat your wives with love and kindness. Verily, you have taken them on the security of God, and their persons are made lawful unto you by the words of God. Free your slaves, following my example, and tell others to do the same. But if they wish to stay with you, see that you feed them with such food as you eat yourselves, and clothe them with the stuff you wear. And if they commit a fault which you are not inclined to forgive, then part from them, for they are the servants of God as you and me, and are not to be treated harshly. Know that we are all equal in the sight of Allah, and journey together in this world as a family of brotherhood and sisterhood. All of us belong to the line of Adam, and Adam was created from dust. This is a gift of knowledge for all who cultivate wisdom and humility. An Arab is no better than a non-Arab, nor is a white better than a black, or a black better than a white, except in piety. Nothing is allowed to a Muslim if it belongs to another, unless it is given freely and willingly, so do not oppress each other. I am leaving behind me two things, the Book of God and my example, if you follow these two, you will never go astray. Spend freely of what is given to you, whether in prosperity or in adversity. Restrain your anger and pardon all, for Allah loves those who do good, as it has been revealed. This Hajj is acceptable to Allah, only if we have love in our hearts for each and every one of God's creatures.

The revelations were the gifts of God's mercy to the Prophet Muhammad which sustained him in his love for his friends, family and mankind. He waited for the revelations as God's divine guidance whenever in need of gleaning truth from under the mounds of lies which burdened his sense of justice and compassion. As was the case in one of his much longed-for revelation when his beloved wife Aisha was unjustly slandered. His agony of the soul and spirit was dispelled when a revelation absolving Aisha of all accusations finally came and he was grateful of the unfolding of truth by God's Grace.

*Lo! who spread the slander are a gang among you. Deem it not a bad thing for you; nay, it is good for you. Unto every man of them will be paid that which he hath earned of the sin; and as for among them who had the greater share therein, his will be an awful doom. Why not the believers, men and women, when ye heard it, think good of their own folk, and say: It is a manifest untruth? Why did they not produce four witnesses? Since they produce not witnesses, they verily are liars in the sight of Allah. Had it not been for the Grace of Allah and His Mercy unto you in this world and Hereafter, an awful doom had overtaken you for that whereof ye murmured. When ye welcomed it with your tongues, and uttered with your mouths that whereof ye had no knowledge, ye counted it a trifle. In the sight of Allah, it is very great. Wherefore, when ye heard it, said ye not: It is not for us to speak of this. Glory be to Thee, O Allah! This is awful calumny. Allah admonisheth you that ye repeat not the like thereof ever, if ye are in truth believers. And He expoundeth unto you His revelations. Allah is Knower, Wise* (Quran 24: 11-18).

*And for those of your women who are guilty of lewdness, call to witness four of you against them. And if they testify to the truth of the allegation, then confine them to the houses until death take them or until Allah appoint for them a way through new legislation.* (Quran 4:15)

*And as for the two of you who are guilty thereof, punish them both. And if they repent and improve, then let them be. Lo, Allah is Relenting, Merciful.* (Quran 4:16)

*Those who forswear their wives must wait four months, then if they change their mind, lo, Allah is Forgiving, Merciful.* (Quran 2: 226)

*O ye who believe! It is not lawful for you forcibly to inherit the women of your deceased kinsmen, nor that ye should put constraint upon them that ye may take away a part of that which ye have given them, unless they be guilty of flagrant lewdness. But consort with them in kindness and live with them in fairness. For if ye hate them it may happen that ye hate a thing wherein Allah hath placed much good.* (Quran 4:19)

*And if ye fear that ye will not deal fairly by the orphans, marry of the women, who seem good to you, two or three or four, and if ye fear that ye cannot*

*do justice to so many, then one only, or the captives that your right hand possess. Thus it is more likely that ye will not do injustice.*
(Quran 4:11)

*And if ye wish to exchange one wife for another and ye have given unto one of them a sum of money however great, take nothing form it. Would ye take it by the way of calumny and open wrong?* (Quran 4:20)

*And all married women are forbidden unto you save those whom your right hand possess. It is decree of Allah for you. Lawful unto you are all beyond those mentioned, so that ye seek them with your wealth in honest wedlock, not debauchery. And those of whom ye seek content marrying them, give unto them their portions as a duty. And there is no sin for you in what ye do by mutual agreement after the duty hath been done. Lo, Allah is ever Wise, Knower.* (Quran 4:24)

*And whoso is not able to afford to marry free, believing women, let them marry from the believing Maids whom your Right Hand Possess. Allah knoweth best concerning your faith. Ye proceed from one another, so wed them by permission of their folk and give unto them their portions in kindness, they being honest, not debauched nor of loose conduct. And if when they are honorably married they commit lewdness they shall incur half of the punishment prescribed for free women in that case. This is for him among you who feareth to commit sin. But to have patience would be better for you. Allah is Forgiving, Merciful.* (Quran 4:25)

## Controversial verses

*Your women are a tilth for you to cultivate, so go to your tilth as ye will and send good deeds before you for your souls. And fear Allah and know that ye will one day meet Him. Glad tidings to believers, O Muhammad.* (Quran 2:223)

Some Muslims have interpreted this verse as if the woman is the possession of man and he has absolute right to treat her as his whim dictates. The above verse clearly states man's role as to educate his wife with the example of his own good deeds. The wife could then transmit good deeds to her offspring by nurturing the seeds of goodness from cradle to maturity so that cycle of noble actions could become the inheritance of all generations. The verse below, sidelined by Muslims, attests to the fact of equality that both men and women have similar rights.

*They your wives are your garment and you are a garment for them.* (Quran 2:187)

*And if he hath divorced her the third time, then she is not lawful unto him thereafter until she had wedded another husband. Then if he divorces her, it is no sin for both of them that they come together again if they consider that they are able to observe the limits of Allah. He manifesteth them for people who have knowledge.* (Quran 2:230)

This verse above is misinterpreted as that a woman divorced for the first time (in reference to the pagan custom when man had to say three times, I divorce you, or you are my mother, and they are divorced) can't marry her former husband until she marries another. Such an interpretation doesn't ring true since after she gets divorced from her second husband, she is allowed to marry her former. Yet, if they are divorced again, the first condition doesn't apply to them and the woman can marry her divorced husband without repeating the process of getting married to another first, then getting divorced? This verse sees the light of reason in a narration from Hadith.

Narrated Maquil bin Yasir: I married my sister to a man and he divorced her and when her days of (iddha) prescribed period were over, the man came again and asked for her hand. But I said to him that I married her to you and favored you with her, but you divorced her. Now you come to ask for her hand again? No, by Allah, she will never go back to you again! That man was not a bad man and his wife wanted to go back to him. So Allah revealed the verse: Do not prevent them (Quran 2:232).

> So I said now I will go to Allah's Messenger, and he married her to him again (Al Bukhari 7:61-O.B.).
> And yet during the lifetime of the Prophet Muhammad, Muslims didn't use this practice of the Pagan custom in divorcing their wives. After the death of the Prophet Muhammad, Muslims incorporated that Pagan custom to divorce their wives for selfish motives which is considered a sin according to the precepts of Sharia. The Caliph Omar ordered

the husband to be whipped who dared pronounce divorce thrice in the same sitting, following the Pagan custom (Abu Rahmani).

*The divorced women must observe upon themselves a waiting period of three menstrual cycles.* (Quran 2:228)

*When ye divorce women, and they reach their term, place not difficulties in the way of marrying their former husbands, if it is agreed between them in kindness. This is an admonition for him among you who believeth in Allah and the Last Day. This is more virtuous for you, and dearer. Allah knoweth, ye know not.* (Quran 2:232)

*Lodge them where ye dwell, according to your wealth and harass them not so as to straiten life for them. And if they are with child, then spend for them till they bring forth their burden. Then if they give suck for you, give them their due payment and consult together in kindness, but if ye make difficulties for one another, then let another woman give suck for the father of the child.* (Quran 65:6)

*Men are in charge of women, because Allah hath made one of them excel the other and because they spend of their property for the support of women. So good women are the obedient, guarding in secret that which Allah hath guarded. As from those whom ye fear rebellion, admonish them and banish them to beds apart, and scourge them. Then if they obey you, seek not a way against them. Lo, Allah is ever High, Exalted, Great!* (Quran 4:34)

Hanifi jurists were the first ones to formulate legal maxims, then Shafiis, Hanbalis and Malikis. As to this highly controversial verse above Maliki jurist Al Arab has stated that *any deliberate act of desertion that is intended to harm and humiliate his wife makes the husband liable to punishment in view of another verse: Live with them in fairness.* (Quran 4:19)

Therefore any act which is harmful and deliberate is enough to violate the Quranic directive on fair treatment.

Another jurist Yusuf al-Qaradawi says that, "Even in the case of the husband proposing divorce, the judge should not order a divorce and advice the husband and admonish him for fear of God and cease harming his wife. In conclusion he states that the husband has violated the spirit of fairness as the Quran has decreed and that he must put an end to abuse."

The Prophet was most emphatic in enjoining upon Muslims to be kind to their women when he delivered his famous Sermon on the

Mount of Mercy at Arafat in the presence of one hundred and twenty-four thousands of his Companions who had gathered there for the Farewell Pilgrimage. In it, he ordered those present, and through them all those Muslims who were to come later, to be kind and respectful toward women.

Prevention of harm is a general goal of Sharia and applies to specific subjects. Examples of the particular goals are those that pertain to any family matters, financial transactions, labor relations, witnessing and adjudication and the like.

The Muslim scholar Shatibi, in his theory of goals, accentuated knowledge of the goals as a prerequisite for attainment of the rank of a scholar. He says those who neglect to acquire mastery of the Islamic goals do so to their own peril as it would make them liable to error in independent reasoning. Included amongst those were the proponents of pernicious innovation who only looked at the apparent text of the Quran without pondering its objective and meaning. These innovators held on to the intricate segments of the Quran and premised their conclusions on them. They took a fragmented and atomized approach to the reading of the Quran which failed to tie up the relevant parts of the texts together.

If Sharia is just hatred, murder, injustice, intolerance and oppression of women, it is not worthy to exist in Islam and must be exterminated along with its claimants steeped deep in the offal of lies and distortion.

# Chapter 3 ~ Sharia for Men

*Allah would make the burden light for you, for man was created weak.* (Quran 4:28)

Is Sharia to be the law of justice, equality, tolerance or compassion? Or is it to be the law of misogyny, injustice, inequality, intolerance, suppression? Muslims have to decide which law to implement.

*And of His signs is this: He created for you helpmates from yourself that ye might find rest in them, and He ordained between you love and mercy. Lo, herein indeed are portents for folk who reflect.* (Quran 30:21)

*And covet not the thing in which Allah hath made some of you excel others. Unto men a fortune from that which they have earned, and unto women a fortune from that which they have earned. Envy not one another, but ask Allah of His bounty. Lo, Allah is Knower of all things.* (Quran 4:32)

*I cast the garment of love over thee from Me. And this in order that thou mayest be reared under Mine Eye.* Quran 20:39)

*Create not disorder on earth.* (Quran 1: 12)

*Work not confusion in earth after the fair ordering thereof, and call on Him in fear and hope. Lo, the mercy of Allah is nigh unto good.* (Quran 7:56)

*The faithful slaves of the Beneficent are they who walk upon the earth modestly, and when the foolish ones address them, answer: Peace.* (Quran 25:63)

*And when it is said unto them: make not mischief in the earth, the say: We are peacemakers only.* (Quran 2:11)

*Wrong not mankind in their goods, and do not evil, making mischief in the earth.* (Quran 26:183)

*Yet whoso doeth evil or wrongeth his own soul, then seeketh pardon of Allah, will find Allah Forgiving, Merciful.* (Quran 4:110)

*Sanction is given to those who fight against you, but begin not hostilities. Lo, Allah loveth not aggressors.* (Quran 2:190)

*O ye who believe! Squander not your wealth among yourselves in vanity, except it be a trade by mutual consent and kill not one another. Lo, Allah is ever merciful to you.* (Quran 4:29)

*Whoso doeth that through aggression and injustice, We shall cast him into Fire, and that is ever easy for Allah.* (Quran 4:30)

*And when we made with you a covenant saying: shed not the blood of your people nor turn a party of your people out of your dwellings. Then you ratified our covenant and you were witnesses thereto.* (Quran 2:84)

*O mankind, call upon your Lord humbly and in secret. Lo, he loveth not aggressors.* (Quran 7:55)

> War is a deceptive error (Prophet Muhammad Al Bukhari LV1:157-3).
>
> The energetic man is not one who uses force, but one who keeps control of himself in a moment of anger (Prophet Muhammad Al Bukhari LXV111:76(1).
>
> The Prophet said, a Muslim is a brother of another Muslim, so he should not oppress him, nor should he hand him over to an oppressor. Whoever fulfilled the needs of his brother, Allah will fulfill his needs. Whoever brought his brother out of discomfort, Allah will bring him out of discomforts on the Day of Resurrection and whoever screened a Muslim, Allah will screen him on the Day of Resurrection (Al Bukhari [3:622-O.B]).
>
> The Prophet said, may I tell you of the people of paradise? Every weak and poor obscure person whom the people look down upon but if he takes an oath to do something, his oath is fulfilled by Allah. And may I inform you of the people of hellfire? They are all those violent, arrogant and stubborn people (Al Bukhari [6:440-O.B]).
>
> The Prophet said, the most hated persons with Allah are three, an evil-doer, a person who seeks the traditions of the Period of Ignorance and a person who seeks to shed somebody's blood without any right (Al Bukhari [9:21-O.B]).
>
> The Prophet said, none of you should point out towards his Muslim brother with a weapon, for he does not know, Satan may tempt him to hit him and thus he would fall into a pit of fire (Al Bukhari [9:193-O.B]).
>
> The Prophet forbade robbery and mutilation of the bodies (Al Bukhari [3:654-O.B]).
>
> Do not become infidels after me by killing each other (Prophet Muhammad/ Al-Bukhari [1:22-OB]).

There are three things of which God disapproves, cunning plans, waste of goods and excessive requests. And three are the enemies of my religion. The fundamentalists, the fundamentalists, the fundamentalists (Prophet Muhammad Al Bukhari XX1V:53(2)).

Since extremists are intent on brutal means of vengeance they themselves don't know for what purpose, these verses below might help young Muslims not to be lured by hate ideology and learn about the gift of forgiveness in the Quran. And get to know God as Merciful God.

## Forgiveness

*Allah Forgiving, Merciful.* (Quran 4:110)

*And O Muhammad say: My Lord, forgive and have mercy, for Thou art best of all who show mercy.* (Quran 23:118)

*For believing men and women, for devout men and women, for humble men and women, for them Allah hath prepared forgiveness and a great reward.* (Quran 33:35)

*Say: O My slaves who have been prodigal to their own hurt! Despair not of the mercy of Allah, Who forgiveth all sins. Lo, He is the forgiving, the merciful.* (Quran 39:53)

*It may be that Allah will ordain love between you and those of them with whom you are at enmity. Allah is mighty, and Allah is Forgiving, Merciful.* (Quran 60:7)

*Ask pardon of your Lord and then turn unto Him repentant. Lo, my Lord is Loving, Merciful.* (Quran 11:90)

*Lo, Allah enjoineth justice and kindness, and giving to kinsfolk, and forbiddeth abomination and wickedness. He exhorteth you in order that ye may take heed.* (Quran 16:90)

*Announce, O Muhammad, unto my slaves that verily I am Forgiving, the Merciful.* (Quran 15:49)

*And if anyone of the idolaters seeketh thy protection O Muhammad, then protect him so that he may hear the word of Allah, and afterward convey him to his place of safety. That is because they are a folk who know not.* (Quran 9:6)

*And for such it may be that Allah will pardon them. Allah is ever Clement, Forgiving.* (Quran 4:99)

*Whereby Allah guideth him who seeketh. His good pleasure into paths of peace. He bringeth them out of darkness unto light by His decree, and guideth them unto a straight path.* (Quran 5:16)

*Forgiveness is only incumbent on Allah toward those who do evil in ignorance and then turn quickly in repentance to Allah. These are they toward whom Allah relenteth. Allah is ever Wise, Knower.* (Quran 4:17)

*The forgiveness is not for those who do ill deeds until, when death attendeth upon one of them, he saith: Lo, I repent now, not yet for those who die while they are disbelievers. For such We have prepared a painful doom.* (Quran 4:18)

*But whoso repenteth after his wrongdoing and amendeth, lo, Allah will relent toward him or her. Lo, Allah is Merciful, Forgiving.* (Quran 5:39)

*Those who spend of which Allah hath given them in ease and in adversity, those who control their wrath and are forgiving toward mankind. Allah loveth the good.* (Quran 3:134)

*And We prescribed for them therein: The life for the life, and the eye for the eye, and the nose for the nose, and the ear for the ear, and the tooth for the tooth, and for wounds retaliation. But whoso forgoeth it in the way of charity, it shall be expiation for him. Whoso judgeth not by that which Allah hath revealed, such are wrong-doers.* (Quran 5:45)

*Verily in the messenger of Allah ye have a good example for him who looketh unto Allah and the Last Day, and remembereth Allah much.* (Quran 33:21)

*Lo, Allah is ever merciful unto you.* (Quran 4:29)

Prophet Muhammad's sayings selected below may teach young Muslim students the precepts of true Islam. May they contemplate goodness and not be disillusioned by lies and distortions paraded so explosively by clerics and hypocrites.

## Prophet's Justice and Kindness

That person is not one of us who inviteth others to aid him in violence.

And he is not one of us who fighteth for his tribe in injustice.

And he is not one of us who dieth in assisting his tribe in tyranny.

The creation is God's family; for its sustenance is from Him. Therefore the most beloved unto God is the person who doeth good to God's family.

Kindness is a mark of faith. And whoever does not kindness hath no faith.

## Controversial verses

*Warfare is ordained for you, though it is hateful unto you, but it may happen that ye hate a thing which is good for you, and it may happen that you love a thing which is bad for you. Allah knoweth, ye know not.* (Quran 2:216)

Jihadists take this verse literally, justifying war. Yet this verse was revealed when Meccans were waging war against the Muslims and the Prophet, being averse to war and always a champion of peace, didn't want to fight with his kinsmen. Yet, in view of several verses in the Quran inclined to peace and forbidding aggression, Muslims are reminded not to promote warfare.

*And slay them wherever you find them, and drive them out of the places whence they drove you out, for persecution is worse than slaughter. And fight not them at the Inviolable Place of Worship until they first attack you there, but if they attack you there then slay them. Such is the reward of disbelievers.* (Quran 2:191)

The extremists love this verse as a sanction for killing, yet this doesn't apply in this time and age when there is no persecution. This verse was revealed when the Prophet and his followers were brutally persecuted, and yet still forbidden to fight near the precincts of Kaaba.

*The only reward of those who make war upon Allah and His Messenger and strive after corruption in the land will be that they will be killed or crucified, or have their hands and feet on alternate sides cut off, or will be expelled out of the land. Such will be their degradation in the world and in the Hereafter theirs will be an awful doom.* (Quran 5:33)

This verse is utterly distorted by the Muslim fundamentalists for the past few decades as a ticket to tyranny and mutilation in defiance to the Prophet's strict injunction against killing and mutilation. This verse was suggestive of harsh punishments when Muslims were on the brink of annihilation by the Meccans along with the assistance of treachery from the hypocrites of Medina, using the word 'reward', not necessarily incurring such punishments. No such punishments were ever inflicted during the life of the Prophet Muhammad, not even by the succession of the Imams and Caliphs.

*They ask thee O Muhammad of the spoils of war. Say: The spoils of war belong to Allah and the messenger, so keep your duty to Allah and adjust the matter of your difference, and obey Allah and His messenger, if you are true believers.* (Quran 8:1)

*When thy Lord inspired the angels, saying, I am with you. So make those who believe stand firm. I will throw fear into the hearts of those who disbelieve. Then smite the necks and smite of them each finger.* (Quran 8:12)

Distortion of verses such as this one began slowly and gradually after the fragmentation of Islam with different sects and schools of thought. Again, this verse doesn't apply to the present day warfare of high-tech weapons. It was revealed at the first battle of Badr when a handful of Muslims were constrained to fight against the large highly trained army of the Meccan. Against great odds, the victory in this battle was a miracle for Muslims when high winds and a dust storm almost blinded the Meccan, resulting in their defeat.

*That is because they opposed Allah and His messenger. Whoso opposeth Allah and His messenger, for him, lo, Allah is severe in punishment.* (Quran 8:13)

*That is the award, so taste it and know that for disbelievers is the torment of the Fire.* (Quran 8:14)

Disbelievers in this case were pagan Arabs bent on destroying the religion of Islam, and fundamentalists have distorted this verse in deeming everyone else infidel who doesn't profess Islam. Again Torment of Fire was a suggested award, not an edict against those who were the tormentors of the Muslims.

*O Prophet! Exhort the believers to fight. If there be of you twenty steadfast they shall overcome two hundred, and if there be of you a hundred steadfast they should overcome a thousand of those who disbelieve, because they are a folk without intelligence.* (Quran 8:65)

Another verse which finds favor with the jihadists is that they are commanded to fight with a promise of overcoming great multitudes, regardless of their own little numbers or resources. This revelation, too, was the product of a problem in that time and age, offering solution to Muslims against the overwhelming assault of the Meccan when their own army was small and ill-equipped.

*O ye who believe! The idolaters only are unclean. So let them not come near the Inviolable Place of Worship after this their year. If ye fear poverty from the loss of their merchandise, Allah shall preserve you of His bounty if He will. Lo, Allah is Wise, Knower.* (Quran 9:28)

Mecca, being the center of trade, attracted tribes from many parts of Arabia whose aim was trading, not worshipping. Their greed and indecent attire became the catapult of this revelation. Now it is misinterpreted as a barrier against all who are not Muslims.

*Fight against such of those who have been given the Scripture as believe not in Allah, nor the Last Day. And forbid not which Allah hath forbidden by His messenger and follow not the religion of truth, until they pay the tribute readily, being brought low.* (Quran 9:29)

Much distorted by the fundamentalists, this revelation has become a window of aggression for the Muslim warriors, though it was also a piece of problem solving for the Muslims when the caravans were being frequently attacked for booty and a treaty was signed between the Jews and the Muslims. The Muslims promised to safeguard their property and merchandise at a certain price since Muslims ruled and were in majority. If the Muslims failed to protect the Jews and Christians, they were not obligated to pay the tribute.

*And the Jews say: Ezra is the son of Allah, and the Christians say: The Messiah is the son of Allah. That is their saying with their mouths. They imitate the saying of those who disbelieved of old. Allah Himself fighteth against them. How perverse are they!* (Quran 9:30)

Preceding this revelation was another revelation in which God commanded the Prophet to change the direction of Qiblah from Jerusalem to Kaaba. The Jews got so angry with the Prophet that they accused him of deception, severing ties with the Muslims and urging the Christians to do the same. The Prophet's followers were scandalized and this verse was a balm to their sense of injury. This verse has also become another tool of distortion into the hands of the orthodox who interpret it as a command to fight against the Jews and the Christians.

*If you go not forth He will afflict you with a painful doom and will choose instead of you a folk other than you. Ye cannot harm Him at all. Allah is able to do all things.* (Quran 9:39)

This revelation was a warning to Muslims who were averse to accompanying the Prophet at the Battle of Ohud where he was constrained to fight with the Meccans. Now extremists use this as a whip of commandment against all Muslims who do not wish to join them in their acts of tyranny and terrorism.

*Those who were left behind rejoiced at sitting still behind the messenger of Allah and were averse to striving with their wealth and their lives in Allah's way. And they said: Go not forth in heat. Say: The heat of hell is more intense of heat, if they but understand.* (Quran 9:81)

*Then let them laugh a little. They will weep much as the reward of what they used to earn.* (Quran 9:82)

The Muslims were defeated at the battle of Ohud and these revelations chided the ones who stayed behind. Yet this revelation becomes another instrument of power into the hands of the jihadists who consign their brethren to hell if they refuse to join them in their madness to kill and destroy.

*O Prophet. Strive against the disbelievers and the hypocrites. Be harsh with them. Their ultimate abode is hell, a hapless journey's end.* (Quran 9:37)

This revelation also belongs to the same time frame as of Battle of Ohud. Some Muslim leaders who had initially started with the Prophet as allies at the head of armies toward the battleground, had deserted and had taken their soldiers back to their safe territories, depleting the number of the soldiers which resulted in defeat for the Muslims. Once again the Prophet's companions were sorely disappointed and were soothed by this revelation. Disregarding the Prophet's injunctions for peace, the extremists use this revelation also to fight and hurl their self-proclaimed enemy to hell.

*If Allah bring thee back from a campaign unto a party of them and they ask of thee leave to go out to fight, then say unto them: Ye shall never more go out with me, nor fight with me against a foe. Ye were content with sitting still, with the useless.* (Quran 9:83)

Another revelation after the Prophet returned from the battle is a reprimand to the Muslims who seemed to have lost the privilege of going with him in his future campaigns.

*Accursed, they will be seized wherever found and slain with a fierce slaughter.* (Quran 33:61)

This revelation is also a specific bubble of time when the Chief of Nejd murdered seventy Muslim men after inviting them on a pretext that he wanted to learn about the precepts of Islam. Fundamentalists use this revelation as a free reign to mass slaughter.

*And never O Muhammad pray for one of them who dieth, nor stand by his grave. Lo, they disbelieved in Allah and His messenger, and they died while they were evil-doers.* (Quran 9:84)

A revelation at the time when the Prophet's eldest daughter Zainab came to Medina, but on the way her carriage was overturned by the raiders of Abu Sofyan, resulting in her miscarriage. Some orthodox Muslims use this revelation as an excuse not to pray for non-Muslims.

*Lo, Allah hath bought from the believers their lives and their wealth because the Garden will be theirs. They shall fight in the way of Allah and shall slay and be slain. It is a promise which is binding on Him on the Torah and the Gospel and the Quran. Who fulfilleth His covenant better than Allah? Rejoice then in your bargain that ye have made, for that is the supreme triumph.* (Quran 9:111)

After the conquest of Mecca a clan of Banu Saad, along with the tribe of Hawazin under the command of Malik ibn Auf, fought against the Muslims, unwilling to acknowledge the Prophet Muhammad as the leader of Mecca. Some of the newly converted Muslims either fought half-heartedly or deserted outright, ignoring the pleas of Al Abbas the uncle of the Prophet, rallying them to return to the battlefield known as the Valley of Hunain. This revelation came as an urgent commandment to Muslims with a promise of heavenly reward. Now, without even a hint of provocation from any quarters, this revelation is used by the Muslims to slay mankind and be slain for the reward of the heaven.

*It is not for the Prophet, and those who believe, to pray for the forgiveness of idolaters even though they may be near of kin to them after it hath become clear that they are people of hell-fire.* (Quran 9:113)

The Prophet Muhammad, the champion of forgiveness, always forgave all pagan Arabs who persecuted him, amongst them his own uncle Abu Lahab. After repeated assaults from Abu Lahab, pelting him with stones and curses, this verse was revealed, though Prophet Muhammad remained faithful to the art of forgiving till his death.

*And whoso seeketh as religion other than the surrender to Allah, it will not be accepted form him, and he will be a loser in the Hereafter.* (Quran 3:85)

This revelation simply proclaims the oneness of God.

*Lo, those who disbelieve after their profession of belief and afterward grow violent in disbelief, their repentance will not be accepted. And such are those who are astray.* (Quran 3:90)

Disbelief didn't demand any punishment, yet this revelation in the hands of the extremists becomes a gateway to murder.

*They long that you should disbelieve, even as they disbelieve, that ye may be upon a level with them. So choose not friends with them till they forsake their homes in the way of Allah. If they turn back to enmity, then take them and kill them wherever you find them and choose no friend nor helper from among them.* (Quran 4:89)

Another time-capsule revelation which can't be applied in any present-day situation. It was revealed after the Meccans many failed attempts to convince the Prophet Muhammad with bribes and honeyed words to abandon his religion of one God. The final attempt transpired after this revelation when seemingly friendly, they concocted a plan to murder him, which also failed since by God's guidance he left Mecca in the night, which became the year of Hijra.

*Lo, those who disbelieve, among the People of the Scripture and the idolaters, will abide in the fire of hell. They are the worst of created beings.* (Quran 98:6)

This revelation is in the same time frame as that of the battle of Ohud when the leaders of some Jewish and Christian tribes broke their treaties of alliance with the Prophet Muhammad and secretly allied with the Meccans—the idolaters with the intention of annihilating the Muslims.

*Whoso disbelieveth in Allah after his belief—save him who is forced thereto and whose heart is still content with the Faith—but whoso findeth ease in disbelief: on them is wrath from Allah. Theirs will be an awful doom.* (Quran 16:106)

Verses such as this were in response to that age and time when breaking of loyalties meant unrest and warfare and in order to avoid such ills of society, harsh punishments were pronounced in revelations. Though Prophet Muhammad himself didn't judge his followers on the basis of such revelations.

*And thou wilt find them greediest of mankind for life and greediest than the idolaters. Each one of them would like to be allowed to live a thousand years. And to live a thousand years would by no means remove him from the doom. Allah is seer of what they do.* (Quran 2:96)

Some of the newly converted Muslims in Medina had begun to think that their faith would grant them long lives. To check that misconception this verse was revealed.

*Yet of mankind are some who take unto themselves objects of worship which they set as rivals to Allah, loving them with a love like that which is due of Allah only. Those who believe are stauncher in their love for Allah. Oh, that those who do evil had but known, on the day when they behold the doom that power belongeth wholly to Allah, and that Allah is severe in punishment.* (Quran 2:165)

Despite the close-knit community of Muslims, a few still persisted in being loyal to their old pagan beliefs, and this verse was revealed as a guide and as an admonishment.

*Let not the believers take disbelievers for their friends in preference to believers. Whoso doeth that hath no connection with Allah unless it be that ye but guard yourselves against them, taking as it were security. Allah biddeth you beware only of Himself. Unto Allah is the journeying.* (Quran 3:28)

The Prophet Muhammad received this revelation after it became clear to him that some of the Muslims in his community trusted pagan Meccans as their friends to such an extent that they were betrayed time and time again without learning the lesson of self-reliance.

*This is because they have chosen the life of the world rather than the Hereafter and because Allah guideth not the disbelieving folk.* (Quran 16:107)

This verse was an answer to the Prophet's hopeless, helpless pain in guiding his people on the path to righteousness.

*The recompense of an injury is an injury equal to it, but if one forgives and makes reconciliation, his reward is with God.* (Quran 42:40)

*As for the thief, both male and female, cut off their hands. It is a reward of their own deeds, an exemplary punishment from Allah. Allah is Wise, Mighty.* (Quran 5:38)

Extremists use only the first part of this verse, sidelining the next, so that they can exact punishment and are not constrained to forgiveness. Also, neglecting to heed the verse above which enjoins forgiveness and reconciliation. The verse below surely enjoins forgiveness.

*And for the thief, male or female, cut off their hands as retribution for their deed and exemplary punishment from God. And God is exalted in power. Most Wise. But one who repents after his crime and amends his conduct, God redeems him. God is Forgiving, Most Merciful.* (Quran 5:38-39)

*And stay quietly in your houses, and make not a dazzling display like that of the former times of ignorance.* (Quran 33:33)

This verse is dear to the hearts of the extremists to confine women within the four walls of their homes. Yet it was revealed after the Prophet Muhammad's wives had complained that men are taking all the merits of courage in defending the religion of Islam, while the women are being cheated of gaining any merits in the realm of religion. The Prophet Muhammad told them that they were already courageous in taking care of their families. They asked how they could earn merit in the Way of Religion and the Prophet's response was to live simply and stay at home to teach children and to write down the revelations.

"Experiments with the imposition of a uniform Sharia have not succeeded in a single country in the past or present and have always resulted in an eruption of public fury and disgust, wiping out even the last remnants of such imposed interference in social and personal matters. People do not think or act in the same manner or talk in the same fashion. A variety of languages, endless dross-differences, contrasting lifestyles and varied cultures mark the original divergence of the human race and reflect silently that every single individual is cast in a different mold. Even father and son or children of the same family, although they are bound by common ties of religion, culture, blood relations and language, yet they have to be provided with different treatment and opportunities by the parents in accordance with their differing aptitudes. Human nature is alike, but the diversity in behavior patterns and tendencies cannot be denied or ignored.

It is man's very personal freedom to take up the life-style he wishes and to execute his matters as he desires. Any mandatory imposition of uniformity in life-style and personal laws, will amount to robbing him of his God-given freedom, for even God does not impose any life-style forcibly on man. Having granted him an intellect, discretion-power and freedom of will, God allowed man the liberty to select from any of the two ways, the satanic way or God-given guidance. While God did not impose uniform laws forcefully on man in view of human intelligence and freedom of will and direction, it is outright blasphemy to talk of man-made authority imposing any kind of man-made law on humans with a blatant disregard for their freedom of will and discretion-powers and intelligence, the very qualities for which God did not thrust any law on man forcibly. Any such whimsical dogmatism of barbaric repression under Sharia can only mean transformation of feeling, thinking human beings into ants or mindless animals that are led by the nose wherever fancy wanders" (Safia Iqbal).

# Chapter 4 ~ Sharia for Jurists

Harm shall neither be inflicted nor reciprocated in Islam."
Hadith
Sharia snatched from the Traditions of the Prophet speaks to the judges in simple terms, stressing that they must remain true to the cause of justice. A small example is when before going to the war the Prophet forbade maiming, injury to women, children and elderly, as well as damage to the animals, and took to task those who caused abuse and hardship.
Aisha was the first female jurist of Islam. Through her, almost one third of Islamic laws were transmitted by the virtue of her sharp memory and intelligence. Laws pertaining to family, marriage, divorce, marital life, succession were related by her with great clarity and precision.
"Any ruling that abandons justice in favor of tyranny, mercy for its opposite, public interest for corruption and wisdom for futility, would have nothing to do with Sharia even if it is shown, by some remote interpretation to be a part of it (Ibn Qayyim).

*O ye who believe, fulfill faithfully all your contracts. (Quran 5:1)*

*Devour not the properties of one another unlawfully, but let there be lawful trade by mutual consent. (Quran 4:29)*

*God commands you to render the trusts to whom they are due and when you judge among people, you judge with justice. (Quran 4:58)*

*O ye who believe. Ward off from yourselves and your families a Fire whereof the fuel is men and stones, over which are set angels strong, severe, who resist not Allah in that which He commandeth them, but do that which they are commanded. (Quran 66:6)*

*Unto the men of a family belongeth a share of that which parents and near kindred leave, and unto the women a share of that which parents and near kindred leave, whether it be little or much—a legal share. (Quran 4:7)*

*They ask thee, O Muhammad, what they shall spend? Say: That which ye spend for good must go to parents and near kindred and orphans and the needy and the wayfarer. And whatsoever good ye do, lo, Allah is aware of it.* (Quran 2: 215)

*Wait they for aught else than that Allah should come down unto them in the shadows of the clouds with the angels? Then the case would be already judged. All cases go back to Allah for judgment.* (Quran 2: 210)

*In case of those who are about to die and leave behind them wives, they should bequeath unto their wives a provision for the year without turning them out, but if they go out of their own accord, there is no sin for you in that which they do of themselves within their rights. Allah is Wise, Mighty.* (Quran 2: 240)

*For divorced women a provision in kindness, a duty for those who ward off evil.* (Quran 2: 241)

*Thus Allah expoundeth unto you His revelations so that ye may understand.* (Quran 2: 242)

*Allah chargeth you concerning the provision for your children. To the male the equivalent of the portion of two females, and if there be women more than two, then theirs is two-thirds of inheritance, and if there be one only then the half. And to his parents a sixth of the inheritance. If he have a son and if he have no son and his parents are his heirs, then to his mother appertaineth the third and if he have brethren, then to his mother appertaineth the sixth, after any legacy he may have bequeathed, or debt hath been paid. Your parents or your children: Ye know not which of them is nearer unto you in usefulness. It is an injunction from Allah. Lo Allah is Wise, Knower.* (Quran 4:11)

*And unto you belongeth a half of that which your wives leave, if they have no child, but if they have a child then unto you fourth of that which they leave, after any legacy they may have bequeathed or debt they may have contracted, hath been paid. And unto them belongeth the fourth of that which ye leave if ye have no child, but if ye have a child then eighth of that which ye leave, after any legacy ye may have bequeathed, or debt ye may have contracted, hath been paid. And if a man and a woman have a distant heir, having left neither child nor parent, and he or she have a sister or a brother, only one on the mother's side, then to each of them twain. The brother and the sister sixth, and they be more than two, then they shall be sharers in the third, after any legacy that may have been bequeathed or debt contacted, not injuring the heirs by willing away more than a third of the heritage hath been paid. A commandment from Allah. Allah is Knower, Indulgent.* (Quran 4:12)

*O ye who believe! Obey Allah and obey the messenger, and those of you who are in authority. And if ye have a dispute concerning any matter, refer it to Allah and the messenger if ye are in truth believers in Allah and the Last Day. That is better and more seemly in the end.* (Quran 4:59)

*As for those who believe in Allah, and hold fast unto Him, them, He will cause to enter into his grace and mercy, and will guide them unto him by a straight road.* (Quran 4:176)

*Yet of mankind are some who make unto themselves objects of worship which they set as rivals to Allah. Loving them with a love like that which is due of Allah only. Those who believe are stauncher in their love for Allah. Oh, that those who do evil had but known, on the day when they behold the doom that power belongeth wholly to Allah and that Allah is severe in punishment.* (Quran 2:165)

*And speak not, concerning that which your own tongues qualify as clean or unclean, the falsehood: this is lawful and this is forbidden? So that ye invent a lie against Allah. Lo, those who invent a lie against Allah will not succeed.* (Quran 16: 116)

*Forbidden unto you for food are carrion and blood and swine flesh, and that which hath been dedicated to any other than Allah, and the strangled. And the dead through beating, and the dead through falling from a height and that which hath been killed by the goring of horns and the devoured of wild beasts, saving that which ye make lawful by the death-stroke, and that which hath been immolated unto idols. And forbidden it is that you swear by the divining arrows. This is an abomination. This day are those who disbelieve in despair of ever harming your religion, so fear them not, fear Me. This day I have perfected your religion for you and completed my favor unto you, and have chosen for you as religion Al-Islam. Whoso is forced by hunger, not by will, to sin: for him, lo, Allah is Merciful, Forgiving.* (Quran 5:3)

*O ye who believe! When you rise up for prayer, wash your faces and your hands up to the elbows and lightly rub your hands and wash your feet up to the ankles. And if ye are unclean, purify yourself. And if ye are sick and on a journey, or one of you cometh from the closet, or you have had contact with women, and ye find not water, then go to clean, high ground and rub your face and your hands with some of it. Allah would not place a burden on you, but He would purify you and perfect you. His grace upon you that ye may give thanks.* (Quran 5:6)

*Allah promiseth you much booty that ye will capture, and hath given you this in advance, and hath withheld men's hands from you that it may be a token for the believers and that He may guide you on a right path.* (Quran 48:20)

*O ye who believe. When you contract a debt for a fixed term, record it in writing. Let a scribe record it in writing between you in terms of equity. No scribe should refuse to write as Allah hath taught him, so let him write and let him who incurreth the debt dictate and let him observe his duty to Allah his Lord, and diminish naught thereof. But if he who oweth the debt is of low understanding or weak or unable himself to dictate, then let the guardian of his interests dictate in terms of equity. And call to witness from among your men, two witnesses. And if two men be not at hand, then a man and two women, of such as ye approve as witnesses, so that if the one erreth through forgetfulness the other will remember. And the witnesses must not refuse when they are summoned. Be not averse to writing down the contract whether it be small or great, with record of the term thereof. That is more equitable in the sight of Allah and more sure for testimony, and the best way of avoiding doubt between you, save only in the case when it is actual merchandise which ye transfer among yourselves from hand to hand. In that case it is no sin for you if ye write it not. And have witnesses when ye sell one to another and let no harm be done to scribe or witness. If ye do harm to them, lo, it is a sin in you. Observe your duty to Allah. Allah is teaching you. And Allah is Knower of all things.* (Quran 2:282)

*O ye who believe! You are forbidden to inherit women against their will. Nor should you treat them with harshness, that they may take away part of the dowry you have given them. Live with them on a footing of equity and kindness. If you take a dislike to them, it may be that you dislike something and Allah will bring about through it a great deal of good.* (Quran 4:19)

*If you fear a break between the two, then appoint two arbiters. One from his family and the other from hers. If they wish for peace, Allah will cause them to reconcile, for Allah hath full knowledge and is acquainted with all things.* (Quran 4: 35)

*And for those who launch a charge against their spouses, and have in support no evidence but their own, their solitary evidence can be received. If they bear witness four times with an oath by Allah that they are solemnly telling the truth. And a fifth oath should be that they solemnly invoke the curse of Allah on themselves if they tell a lie. But it would avert punishment from the wife if she bears witness four times with an oath by Allah that her husband is telling a lie. And the fifth oath should be that she solemnly invokes the wrath of Allah on herself if her husband is telling the truth.* (Quran 24: 5-9)

*For Muslim men and women, for believing men and women, for devout men and women, for true men and women. For men and women who are patient and constant, for men and women who humble themselves, for men and women who give in charity, for men and women who fast, for men and women who guard their chastity. And for men and women who engage much in Allah's praise, for them has Allah prepared great reward and forgiveness.* (Quran 33: 35)

*The alms are only for the poor and the needy and those who collect them, and those whose hearts are to be reconciled and for those in Bondage and the debtors and for the cause of Allah and for the wayfarer, a duty imposed by Allah. Allah is Knower, Wise.* (Quran 9:60)

> Some of the companions of Prophet said to him: Messenger of God, the rich have born away the rewards. They pray as we do, fast as we do, and besides they make alms with the surplus of their wealth. The Prophet Answered: And how has God not given you wherewithal to make alms? To say Glory to God is an alms, to say God is most great is an alms. Whatever you bid to the good is an alms, when you reject the disapproved it is an alms. Each time you perform the conjugal act, it is an alms. They said: What? We can satisfy our fleshly appetites and gain a reward? The Prophet answered: Is not the one who satisfies his appetites illicitly guilty of a sin? Just so, one who satisfies them lawfully gains a reward (Muslim/Al).

Narrated ibn Abbas that Hilal bin Umaiya accused his wife of committing sexual intercourse with Sharik bin Sahma and filed the case before the Prophet.

> The Prophet said: Either you bring forth a proof of four witnesses or you would receive the legal punishment of eighty lashes on your back. The woman was allowed to take oaths of her innocence and when she did and her oaths were considered genuine against her husband's and she didn't receive any punishment (Al Bukhari [6:271-O.B]).

Allah's Messenger said: In Paradise there is a pavilion made of single hollow pearl sixty miles wide, in each corner of which there are wives who will not see those in the other corners, and the believers will visit and enjoy them. Al Bukhari [6:402-O.B.]

The Prophet said: A matron should not be given in marriage except after consulting her, and a virgin should not be given in marriage except after her permission (Al Bukhari [7:67-O.B.]).

If a man gives his daughter in marriage while she is averse to it, then such marriage is invalid. Narrated Khuns bint Khidham that her father gave her in marriage when she was a matron and she disliked her marriage. So she went to Allah's Messenger, and he declared that marriage invalid (Al Bukhari [7:69-O.B.]).

Hisham ibn Urwa relates on the authority of Abu Saliih from Abu Huraira that the Messenger of God said: Other rulers will govern you after me. The pious will govern you with his piety, and the libertine with his immorality. Listen to them both, and obey them in everything that conforms with the truth. If they do well, it is to their credit and yours, but if they do evil, it will be to your credit and their discredit. The persons to govern should follow these rules: Justice in all its characteristics. Knowledge requisite for independent judgments about legal matters which is revealed. Soundness of the senses in sight, speech and hearing, in a degree to accord with their normal functioning. Soundness of the members from any defect which would prevent freedom of agility and movement. Judgment conducive to governing the subjects and administering matters of general welfare (Hadith).

The Islamic Law orders men to do good and reject what is reprehensible, and it is also obligatory for Muslims to enjoin right behavior on their fellows and deter them from wrong action (Al-amr bi al-Maruf).

## Prophet's Quranic justice and jurisprudence

I am but a human being. When you bring a dispute to me, some of you may be more eloquent in stating their case than others. I may consequently adjudicate on the basis of what I hear. If I adjudicate in favor of someone a thing that belongs to his brother, let him not take it. For it would be like taking a piece of fire.

*It was by the mercy of Allah that thou wert lenient with them, O Muhammad, for if thou hast been stern or fierce of heart they would have dispersed from round about thee. So pardon them and ask forgiveness for them and consult with them upon the conduct of affairs. And when thou art resolved, then put thy trust in Allah. Lo, Allah loveth those who put their trust in Him.* (Quran 3: 159)`

*And those who answer the call of their Lord and establish worship, and whose affairs are a matter of counsel and who spend what We have bestowed on them.* (Quran 42: 38)

*Stand firmly for justice in witness to God even if it be against yourselves, your parents or your relatives, and whether it be against the rich or poor, for God can best protect both. Follow not the lust of your hearts lest it distract you from the course of justice.* (Quran 4:135)

*Whoever is aggressive toward you, then your response must be proportionate to aggression that was inflicted on you.* (Quran 2:194)

*Everyone is accountable for his own deeds, and no soul shall bear the burden of another.* (Quran 6:164)

*We revealed to you the scripture with the truth that you may judge between people by that which God has shown to you, and do not be a pleader for the treacherous.* (Quran 4:105)

*Whoever commits a sin only makes him liable for it, and whoever commits a delinquency and throws the blame thereof upon the innocent, he has burdened himself with falsehood and a flagrant crime.* (Quran 4:111-112)

*They question thee about strong drink and games of chance. Say: In both is great sin and some utility for men, but the sin of them is greater than their usefulness. And they ask thee what they ought to spend. Say: that which is superfluous. Thus Allah maketh plain to you His revelations, that haply ye may reflect.* (Quran 2: 219)

A few of Prophet's sayings below about justice and jurisprudence quoted by Mohammad Hashim Kamali

> When the litigant presents himself before you, do not pass a judgment unless you hear the other party in the same way as you hear the first.
>
> The burden of proof is on him who makes the claim, whereas the oath denying the charge is to him who denies.
>
> If men were to be granted what they claim, some will claim the lives and properties of others.
>
> Every one of you is like a shepherd, and every one of you is responsible for his flock. The ruler is a shepherd and so is the husband, who is responsible for his family. A woman is a shepherd who looks after her husband's household and his children. Thus, every one of you is a shepherd, and every one of you is responsible for his flock.
>
> Be kind to your children and give them a proper education.
>
> Be kind to your daughters, as I also am the father of daughters.
>
> He is not one of us who is not kind to children.
>
> Obey your parents and treat them kindly, for if you do, then your own children will be obedient and kindly to you.
>
> May the mercy of God be on one who is lenient when he sells, lenient when he buys, and lenient when he makes a demand.
>
> A juristic conclusion drawn from these guidelines by the Prophet is that bringing ease to the people and removal of hardship from them is one of the cardinal objectives of Sharia. Hence it is not permissible for a judge or a jurist to opt for a harsh verdict in cases where an easier alternative can be found (Mohammad Hashim Kamali).

*And the firmament has He raised high and set up therein the fine balance in order that you do not transgress the balance. So establish weight with justice and detract not from the divinely ordained balance.* (Quran 55:7-9)

Cited below are a few notes from the book *Siraat-E-Mustaqeem* on jurisprudence:

> Social justice is that aspect of the Law where justice is straightforward and easy of attainment, and an order where

there are equal opportunities for all to progress according to their abilities.

No group can be called just unless it becomes the means of insuring great resources for the progress and betterment of all sections of mankind. A community having a sense of social justice will look after the needs of the entire populace, keeping in mind collective needs without any favor or prejudice, then it will pass as a just community, otherwise it would become a pothole of tyranny.

In social justice, it is the duty of every individual member of the society to co-operate with the society toward this end, to the best of his ability. If a city is in need of a hospital, it is incumbent upon community members, whether they be poets, politicians or journalists to use their talents to convince the rulers to build a hospital.

Therefore if the individuals of any community are shrinking from their duty, the whole community will stand condemned for sin and tyranny. The community is like a body, the individual and the community suffers the same fate.

Equality before Law: In the eyes of the Law the rich and poor, the rustic and the well-groomed and high and low all are equal. That is, whoever commits a crime will be liable to punishment without regard to class or status. There will be no discrimination in legislation.

Equality in Rights: This means that the right to live and the right to freedom be universal, and all benefit equally from these rights. No individual should enjoy any privilege or distinction in this regard.

Equality in Posts and Office: By this it is meant that post and office should not be reserved for any particular community. Whichever individual possesses the qualification for the post should be eligible.

Social justice means that there should be no distinction and privilege as regards basic rights of any human being. They should have the right to vote, and no party should receive special treatment, the rights of rich and poor should be equal.

Muslim jurists contend that the fundamental rule of Law is liberty, but since human nature is weak, easily led astray, covetous and ungrateful, it is necessary both in the interests of the individual and in those of the social organism to set certain limits to human freedom of action in a sense of legal ordinance.

## Safia Iqbal's thoughts on women's rights:

The ceaseless talk of women's rights down the ages, testifies that the rights of women have been trampled in every period of history in one or other part of the world. It is self-deception to believe that women are emancipated today. In fact they are as helpless as suppressed and bound to age-old customs and second class status as they were in the earliest ages. Irrespective of religion, women have always been crushed down socially. Even Muslim women who are entitled to maximum rights in Islam are today steeped in the filth of indignity and degradation. The Muslim community, by shutting its eyes, cannot ignore the harsh reality the rights and status guaranteed by Islam to women, are confined only to the books of Islamic jurisprudence. In practical life, most Muslim women do not get even thirty percent of their rights. This is an ugly fact, a hard fact. A live community, if it wishes to preserve itself and its identity, must have the honesty and daring to face its lapses squarely. Is it not true that Muslims have made a mockery of Islamic laws pertaining to divorce, polygamy, etc.? The ignorance of many has turned bewildered woman into a testing ground for jests and dramas of triple divorce, mock marriages and outrageous laws of oppression.

The Muslim community has itself to blame for the abysmal fall of the Muslim women. Is it not a fact that in some parts of the world even elementary education is denied to the Muslim girls, whereas the Prophet held the attainment of education compulsory for men and women? Is it not true that Muslim girls are often not consulted in the matter of their marriage and not even allowed to see the future life-partner whereas the Prophet has sanctioned that they see each other before getting married? Is it also not true that the bride is almost never consulted by the parents while fixing the dower at the time of marriage whereas she is solely entitled to fix the amount and conditions of her dower as per the Sharia? Adding insult to injury, the dower has been turned into a decoration piece and is not paid to her by the husband whereas the Prophet strongly stressed the payment of dower to the bride? Is it not true that the question of dower rises only upon divorce or death when the husband meekly requests relinquishment of dower by the wife?

With regard to the implementation of penalties, the Prophet instructed the rulers and judges to suspend the prescribed punishment as far as you can. For it is better to err in forgiveness than making an error in punishment.

In a Hadith narrated by Aisha and recorded by both Muslim and Al Bukhari, the Prophet said: God is gentle and He loves gentleness in all matters. Then he confirmed that in another Hadith to say that gentleness fails not to bring beauty in everything and it is not taken away from anything without causing ugliness.

# Chapter 5 ~ Scriptures as One Whole

"The outward Kaaba Ibrahim did built. The inward Kaaba was as the Lord Almighty willed" (Abdullah Al-Ansari).

The first Sura of Quran is the opening of Scripture, also called Lord's Prayer. This Sura below is the essence of Quran since it is recited in public and private worship by all Muslims. Historians assert that it was revealed during the fourth year of the Prophet's Mission and since then it has been used in all prayers.

*In the name of Allah, the Beneficent, the Merciful*
*Praise be to Allah, Lord of the Worlds*
*The Beneficent, the Merciful*
*Owner of the Day of Judgment*
*Thee alone we worship, Thee alone we ask for help*
*Show us the straight path*
*The path of those whom Thou hast favored*
*Not the path of those who earn Thine anger nor of those who go astray.*
(Quran 1:1)

The Sura five in the Quran is also called The Table Spread since a few of its verses are about how the disciples of the Jesus asked that a table be spread with food from the Heaven. These verses below are seen as an allusion to Eucharist.

*When the disciples said: O Jesus, son of Mary! Is thy Lord able to send down for us a table spread with food from heaven? He said: Observe your duty to Allah, if ye are true believers.* (Quran 5: 112)

*They said: we wish to eat thereof, that we may satisfy our hearts and know that thou hast spoken truth to us, and that thereof we may be witnesses.* (Quran 5: 113)

*Jesus, son of Mary said: O Allah, Lord of us! Send down for us a table spread with food from heaven, that it may be a feast for us, for the first of us and for the last of us, and a sign from Thee. Give us sustenance, for Thou art the Best of Sustainers.* (Quran 5:114)

*Allah said: Lo, I send it down for you. And whoso disbelieveth of you afterward, him surely will I punish with a punishment wherewith I have not punished any of My creatures.* (Quran 5: 115)

*And when Allah said: O Jesus, son of Mary! Didst thou say unto mankind: Take me and my mother for two gods beside Allah? Jesus said: Be glorified, it was not mine to utter that to which I had no right. If I used to say it, Thou knowest it. Thou knowest what is in my mind, and I know not what is in Thy Mind. Lo, Thou only, only Thou art the Knower of Things Hidden?* (Quran 5: 116)

*I spake unto them only that which Thou commandest me, saying: Worship Allah, my Lord and your Lord. I was a witness of them while I dwelt among them, and when Thou tookest me Thou wast the Watcher over them. Thou art Witness over all things.* (Quran 5: 117)

*If Thou punish them, lo, they are Thy slaves. And if Thou forgive them, lo, they are Thy slaves. Lo, Thou only, only Thou art the Mighty, the Wise.* (Quran 5: 118)

*Allah saith: This is a day in which their truthfulness profiteth the truthful, for theirs are Gardens underneath which rivers flow, wherein they are secure forever, Allah taking pleasure in them and they in Him. That is the great triumph.* (Quran 5: 119)

*Unto Allah belongeth the Sovereignty of the heavens and the earth and whatsoever is therein, and He is Able to do all things.* (Quran 5: 120)

Jonah is the title of the tenth Sura in the Quran, deriving its name from the verses talking about the folks of Jonah.

*These are the verses of wise Scripture.* (Quran 10: 2)

*If only there had been a community that believed and profited by its belief as did the folk of Jonah! When they believed We drew off from them the torment of disgrace in the life of the world and gave them comfort for a while.* (Quran 10: 99)

*And if thy Lord willed, all who are in the earth would have believed together. Wouldst thou Muhammad compel men until they are believers?* (Quran 10: 100)

*It is not for any soul to believe save by the permission of Allah. He hath set uncleanness upon those who have no sense.* (Quran 10: 101)

During the lifetime of the Prophet Muhammad the Quran existed as an oral entity only. In the Year 650 it was written down in a book form by the orders of the third Caliph Uthman. By that time many of the reciters of the Quran and close companions of the Prophet Muhammad who had transmitted Quran orally had died in battles during the expansion of Islam. However, some of the texts were written down for the purpose of the prayer and worship, so Caliph Uthman employed scholars to collect those texts from all over the Islamic empire. Several versions of the texts were discovered and supposedly destroyed by the scholars, but many variants survived, later commented by the scholars both Muslims and non-Muslims.

Uthman was made aware of the fluctuations of the suras in those texts so he commanded a solid order in arranging suras which could serve as a standard for writing down the book of the Quran. Fragments of the Quran were gathered from all over Arabia and inserted at appropriate places in the texts written by the oral transmitters. When the standard text of the Quran was written down, it only had consonants without any vowels and some were not clearly distinguishable. The Quran had become a piece of contention and several disputes erupted forth as to the vocalization of the text.

Finally, in Year 900 an agreement was reached by the scholars that the Quran was revealed according to seven sets of readings which were equally authentic. Those were validated by the names of the seventh and eighths century scholars, each of whom had two transmitters, whose versions were slightly different. So fourteen different sets of readings were produced, but a complete script was at hand and the readings could be set down precisely and accurately. Consensus was reached that the differences between the sets were negligible and the general meaning of the verse had remained intact. Only one set of reading survived as that of Hafs, transmitted from Asim, later adopted in the standard Egyptian printed edition, first published in Year 1924.

The first century of Islam found the Muslims in possession of a great empire, in newly conquered Persia, Syria, Egypt, North Africa and Mesopotamia. The conquered People of the Book with their own Holy Scriptures were allowed to retain their old religions with the payment of tribute money. And the conquering Arabs dwelt apart in new garrison cities, supported by the taxation money and the booty from their continued campaigns. They surrounded themselves with slaves and captive concubines, and lived on a scale of luxury unknown to their ancestors. There was a strong temptation to regard themselves as a chosen people, and while some of the conquered adopted Islam, the lack of equality accorded them by the Arabs was a source of constant discontent (John Alden Williams).

*Lord grant guidance to my people, for surely they know not.* (Quran 7: 199)

*Lo, my protecting friend is Allah who revealeth the Scripture. He befriendeth the righteous.* (Quran 7: 196)

*He hath revealed unto thee, Muhammad, the Scripture with the truth, confirming that which was revealed before it, even as He revealed the Torah and the Gospel.* (Quran 3:3)

*And unto thee have We revealed the Scripture with the truth, confirming whatever Scripture was before it, and a watcher over it. So judge between them by that which Allah hath revealed, and follow not their desires away from the truth which hath come unto thee. For each we have appointed a divine law and a traced-out way. Had Allah willed, He would have made you one community. But that He may try you by that which He hath given you, He hath made you as you are. So vie one with another in good works. Unto Allah ye will all return, and He will then inform you of that wherein ye differ.* (Quran 5:48)

*Lo, those who believe in that which is revealed unto thee, Muhammad, and those who are Jews, and Christians, and Sabaeans—whoever believeth in God and the Last Day and doeth right—surely their reward is with their Lord, and there shall be no fear come upon them, neither shall they grieve.* (Quran 2:62)

*He hath ordained for you that religion which He commanded unto Noah, and which We inspire in thee Muhammad, and that which we commended unto Abraham and Moses and Jesus, saying: Establish the religion and be not divided therein. Allah chooseth for Himself whom He will, and guideth unto Himself him who turneth toward Him.* (Quran 42: 13)

*This is it which Allah announceth unto His bondmen who believe and do good works. Say O Muhammad unto mankind: I ask of you no fee thereof, save loving-kindness among kinsfolk. And whoso scoreth a good deed We add unto its good for him. Lo, Allah is Forgiving, Responsive.* (Quran 42: 23)

*And verily We gave the children of Israel the Scripture and the Command and the Prophethood, and provided them with good things and favored them above all people.* (Quran 45: 16)

*And gave them plain commandments. And they differed not until after the knowledge came unto them through rivalry among themselves. Lo, thy Lord will judge between them on the Day of Resurrection concerning wherein they used to differ.* (Quran 45:17)

*And now have We set thee O Muhammad on a clear road of Our commandment, so follow it, and follow not the whims of those who know not.* (Quran 45: 18)

*How they come unto thee for judgment when they have the Torah, wherein Allah hath delivered judgment for them? Yet even after they turn away. Such folk are not believers.* (Quran 5:43)

*O People of the Scripture! Now hath our messenger come unto you, expounding unto you much of that which ye used to hide in the Scripture, and forgiving much. Now hath come unto you light from Allah and a plain Scripture.* (Quran 5:15)

*With clear proofs and writings, and We have revealed unto thee the Remembrance that thou mayest explain to mankind that which hath been revealed for them, and that haply they may reflect.* (Quran 16:44)

*Lo, this Quran guideth unto that which is straightest, and giveth tidings unto the believers who do good works that theirs will be a great reward.* (Quran 17:9)

*And He it is Who sendeth down the saving rain after they have despaired, and spreadest out His mercy. He is the Protecting Friend, the Praiseworthy.* (Quran 42: 28)

*And strive for Allah with the endeavor which is His right. He hath chosen you and hath not laid upon you in religion any hardship, the faith of your father Abraham is yours. He hath named you Muslims of old time and in this Scripture that the messenger may be a witness against mankind. So establish worship, pay the poor-due, and hold fast to Allah. He is your Protecting Friend. A blessed Patron and a blessed Helper!* (Quran 22:78)

*And lo, there is a party of them who distort the Scripture with their tongues that ye may think that what they say is from the Scripture, when it is not from the Scripture. And they say: it is from Allah, when it is not from Allah, and they speak a lie concerning Allah knowingly.* (Quran 3:78)

*Verily in the messenger of Allah ye have a good example for him who looketh unto Allah and the Last Day and remembereth Allah much.* (Quran 33:21)

*The way of blame is only against those who oppress mankind, and wrongfully rebel in the earth. For such there is a painful doom. (Quran 42: 42)*

*And those who shun the worst of sins and indecencies and, when they are worth, forgive. (Quran 42: 37)*

*And verily who is patient and forgiveth — lo, that verily is of steadfast heart of things. (Quran 42: 43)*

*And it was not vouchsafed to any mortal that Allah should speak to him unless it be by revelation or from behind a veil, or that He sendeth a messenger to reveal what He will by His leave. Lo, He is Wise, Exalted. (Quran 42: 51)*

*And thus have We inspired in thee O Muhammad a Spirit of Our command. Thou knewest not what the Scripture was, what the Faith. But We have made it a light whereby We guide whom We will of our bondmen. And, lo, thou verily dost guide unto a right path. (Quran 42: 52)*

The Quran and the Tradition are not, as it is often said, the basis of Islamic legal speculation, but only its sources. The real foundation is to be sought in the attitude of mind which determines the methods of utilizing these sources. To say that Quran and Hadith are accepted as infallible sources because they are the title-deeds and foundation of Islam is to argue in a circle. The ultimate reason is metaphysical. It is a conviction of the imperfection of the human reason and its inability to apprehend by its sole powers the real nature of Good or indeed any reality whatsoever. Absolute good and evil therefore be known to men only through a divine revelation mediated through the Prophets. By Divine Providence there has been a succession of such Prophets ever since by the creation of Adam, mankind has existed on this earth. The revelations accorded by these Prophets were all identical in principle, but formed a gradually developing series adapted to the stages of man's development. Each in turn expanded, modified and abrogated the preceding revelations.

Law in the eyes of the Muslim scholars was not in fact an independent or empirical study. It was the practical aspect of the religious and social doctrine taught by the Prophet Muhammad. For the early Muslims there was little or no distinction between legal and religious. In the Quran these two aspects are found side by side, or rather intertwined one with the other, and so likewise in the Hadith.

The study and interpretation of the Quran involved sometimes the one and sometimes the other, and nearly a century elapsed before scholars began to specialize in one or the other aspect. These aspects were distinguished by terms:

Ilm—positive knowledge. Fiqh—understanding.

In the earlier historical traditions about Prophet Muhammad no special care was taken in their transmission, the substance being more important than the precise form of words. Oral transmission was indispensable in view of the primitive state of the Arabic script, although individuals might have made written notes of hadiths for their own use. Within two or three generations however large numbers of hadiths came into circulation, professing to relate statements made by the Prophet on points of law and doctrine. Religious and political parties showed a suspicious readiness to produce sayings of the Prophet in defense of their particular tenants, and as time went on these became more and more detailed and categorical. It was in fact obvious that the Tradition was being invaded by forgeries on a vast scale, sometimes by editing and supplementing genuine old traditions, more often by simple inventions (H. A. R Gibb).

> Allah has given every person the capacity to discern good from evil and the conscience of every man knows and feels this. It is said that to treat well and gently with people is a form of worship, the purpose of all worship. When a person performs a good deed which gives him peace and happiness, it could be safely understood that it is a good deed. Similarly if a person feels sad or repentant after some deed, it is correct to assume that it is sinful. Seek peace of the heart and stay away from restlessness so that life may bloom and be pleasant (Hadith).
>
> The Prophet said: By Allah, he does not believe! By Allah, he does not believe! It was said, who is that, O Messenger of Allah? And Prophet said: That person whose neighbor does not feel safe from his evil (Al Bukhari [8:45-O.B.]).
>
> Allah's Messenger said: Whosoever believes in Allah and the Last Day should not harm his neighbor, and whosoever believes in Allah and the Last Day should entertain his guest generously and whosoever believes in Allah and the Last Day should talk

what is good or keep quiet. Abstain from all kinds of evil and dirty talk, lying, abusing, backbiting, etc. (Al Bukhari [8:47-O.B.]).

Allah's Messenger said: Do not hate one another, and do not be jealous of another, and do not desert each other. O, Allah's worshipers, be brothers. Lo, it is not permissible for any Muslim not to talk to his brother for more than three days (Al Bukhari [8:91-O.B.]).

The Prophet said: Beware of suspicion, for suspicion is the worst of false tales, and do not look for the other's faults and do not spy, and do not be jealous of one another, and do not cut your relations with one another, and do not hate one another. O, Allah's worshipers, Allah has ordered you to be brothers (Al Bukhari [8:90-O.B.]).

A man said to Prophet: advise me. The Prophet said: Do not become angry and furious. The man asked again and the Prophet repeated, do not become angry and furious (Al Bukhari [8:137-O.B.]).

Narrated Ubai bin Kab, Allah's Messenger said: Some poetry contains wisdom (Al Bukhari [8:166-O.B.]).

Narrated Abu Huraira, Allah's Messenger said: whoever recites Kalima one hundred times a day will get the same reward as given for manumitting ten slaves, and one hundred good deeds will be written in his account, and one hundred sins will be deducted from his accounts and it will be a shield for him from Satan on that day till night, and nobody will be able to do a better deed except the one who does more than he (Al Bukhari [8:412-O.B.]).

The Prophet said: When Allah created the Creation He wrote in His Book that is placed on the Throne with Him—and he prescribed for Himself: Verily, My Mercy has overcome My anger (Al Bukhari [9:501-O.B]).

Perfect mercy is pouring out benefaction to those in need, and directing it to them, for their care, and inclusive mercy is when it embraces deserving and undeserving alike. The mercy of God great and glorious is both perfect and inclusive, perfect inasmuch as it wants to fulfill the needs of those in need and does meet them, and inclusive inasmuch as it embraces both deserving and undeserving, encompassing this world and the next, and includes bare necessities and needs, and special gifts over and above them. So He is truly and utterly merciful (Al Ghazali).

Quranic verses are explicit in dealing with the rights of women and so are the prophetic traditions. Quoted below are a few of the Islamic laws recorded in Hadiths attributed to the Prophet Muhammad.

A woman's property is her own and cannot be seized by her husband.

Women cannot be denied the right to education.

Ruining a woman's reputation is a punishable offense.

A woman cannot be forced into marriage.

Women can file legal suits and testify in court.

Women can freely enter into contracts.

Women can divorce their husbands.

Aisha, the Prophet Muhammad's youngest wife survived fifty years after his death and transmitted more than two thousand of the sayings of the Prophet, now recorded in several Hadiths. She memorized all the revelations by heart and acquired knowledge in law, poetry, medicine and the mathematics. She took active part in social reform and education, teaching boys and girls in her home which became her school of learning. Even the caliphs consulted her when in doubt about the meaning of certain words. On the issues of Jihad, she recited the oft-repeated saying of the Prophet Muhammad, regretfully sidelined by scholars and historians and now by the extremists.

*Jihad is not taking a sword and fighting on the way of God. Jihad is taking care of your parents and children and being free from needing others.* Prophet Muhammad

Sharia as a whole in the realm of spirituality is explained below in its perfection through the contemplations of Hazrat Inayat Khan who came from India to America Year 1910 to unite East with the West in the concept of God Realization.

He called the first stage of Sharia as Shariat, meaning when man is impressed by the idea of God-ideal and begins to look up to Him as the light of Guidance. That is when he learns to please all living creatures, earning in return the pleasure of God.

The second stage is called Tariqat. Man arrives at this stage when he begins to see within a host of his own faults which before he saw only in others. At this stage man begins to hone his perception in finding the kernel of unity in all creation.

If one is able to gain sufficient inner knowledge from the second stage, one enters the third stage known as Haqiqat—literally meaning, knowing the truth, even though truth is a relative term according to one's own ability to perceive or experience. At this stage he begins to realize each heart is the shrine of God, not ever to be desecrated.

The last stage is called Marifat. One can only arrive at this stage when realization dawns upon one like a bolt of lightning that Truth and God is One, only to be experienced, not explained.

In essence Sharia needs only the wand of love to transform itself from hate to harmony.

# Chapter 6 ~ Sharia Literally

*You are all the children of Adam and Adam was created from dust.*
Prophet Muhammad

It is likely that in origin the Hadiths as a corpus resembled a ball of many colored threads. There was, of course, the Hadith from the Prophet's wives, but there were also Hadiths, individual units from the Prophet's prominent companions, and quite a lot of them, in addition to the ancient lore and the Near Eastern wisdom. Many individual Hadiths flatly contradict each other. They differ greatly in legal import. Thus the earlier Hadith contained a mass of legal injunctions, ritual practice, ethical conduct, correct manners, admonitions, homilies, fragments of the Prophet's biography, Hadiths about the Last Hour, and virtues of various individuals. In the course of the 9th Century, and coinciding with the bureaucratization of the Muslim scholarship under the Abbasids, the Hadith was systemized in standard collections that remain unchanged to this day. Six of those quickly gained authority and two gained special prestige, those of Al Bukhari (870) and Muslim (875).

Besides the scribes and scholars of the Quran and Hadiths, the writers of Sira—Prophet Muhammad's biographers emerged as historians. The historian was primarily a transmitter, not a critic. Hence inclusion rather than exclusion was the dominant method. Even if a story was unbelievable or inappropriate, it might still be included because it might have moral or aesthetic aspect. The Sira writers took for granted the preponderant role of the supernatural. Hence strange causes of event were tolerated and by extension, strange or unusual evidence could be admitted. There was in addition a different conception of evidence, for example, verse was regarded then as we might record documentary evidence today. The Sira writers operated within a prophetic framework. Muhammad's life needed to be conformed to the life of prophecy as understood by those writers, and needed of course to conform to the Quran (Tarif Khalidi).

A Muslim should be first of good nature, kind and hospitable, the qualities which the Prophet Muhammad himself possessed. If we just give people logical discussions, they may agree with us, but then go away and forget the whole thing because they haven't actually seen you do anything. Aisha said that the Prophet was the Quran walking. This is the key. It is no use reading the Quran—the Quran is the embodiment of the teaching of Allah. Almighty has sent this Quran for the perfection of man, so you can't just use it as a mouthpiece, you must put it into practice. That means say little but do much. Always remember, it is only Allah Who can guide a person to Islam (Al Ghazali).

## Words divine and literal:

Allah: The Arabic name for the God of all nations and of all peoples
Islam: The religion of peace and reconciliation
Jihad: To conquer the forces of evil within one's own self. "Islamic tradition does not have a notion of holy war. Jihad simply means to strive hard or struggle in pursuit of a just cause. Holy war is not an expression used by the Quranic text or Muslim theologians. In Islamic theology war is never holy, it is either justified or not" (Robert Spencer).
Muslim: The one who surrenders to the will of God
Surrender—Striving after righteousness as an act of total submission to the power of goodness in one's own mind and heart.

Concern over the authority of the Sunnah became prominent during the second generation of successors at a time when forgery in Hadith became widely known (Abu Zahrah).

One who seeks knowledge without proof is like a gatherer of wood who goes into the woods at night to collect fallen branches and is bitten by a snake as it was unknowingly taken for another branch. When you find the Sunnah of the Messenger of God opposing what I might have said, follow it and abandon my word. My opinion is correct with the possibility of it being wrong. An opinion different from mine is wrong with the possibility that it is correct (Al Shafi).

The consensus and divergence amongst Muslim scholars of four Schools of Thought have several disagreements. Concerning the Quran the jurists have disagreed over the abrogation of some of the Quranic verses by others where two verses provide divergent ruling on the same subject, or when the Hadith arguably overrules the Quranic verse. While Al Shafi's doctrine of abrogation is based on the rule that Quran can only be abrogated by the Quran and Sunnah only by Sunnah, the other three schools add that the Quran and the Sunnah may also abrogate one another (Mohammad Hashim Kamali).

"Disagreement of my community is a source of mercy. If you love God, love God's creatures first." Prophet Muhammad

*Tell those who believe to forgive those who hope not for the days of Allah. In order that he may requite folk what they used to earn.* (Quran 45: 14) *Confound not truth with falsehood, nor knowingly conceal the truth.* (Quran 2:42)

*It is not for believer to kill a believer unless it be by mistake.* (Quran 4:92) *Whoso slayeth a believer of set purpose, his reward is hell forever. Allah is wrath against him and He hath cursed him and prepared for him an awful doom.* (Quran 4:93)

*The good deed and the evil deed are not alike. Repel the evil deed with one which is better, then lo, he, between whom and thee there was enmity will become as though he was a bosom friend.* (Quran 41:34)

*And each one hath a goal toward which he turneth; so vie with one another in good works. Wheresoever you may be, Allah will bring you all together. Lo, Allah is able to do all things.* (Quran 2:148)

*Those who have been driven from their homes unjustly only because they said: Our Lord is Allah. For had it not been for Allah's repelling some men by means of others, cloisters and churches and oratories and mosques, wherein the name of Allah is oft-mentioned, assuredly would have been pulled down. Verily Allah helpeth one who helpeth Him. Lo, Allah is Strong, Almighty.* (Quran 22: 40)

*And seek the abode of the Hereafter in that which Allah hath given thee and neglect not thy portion of this world, and be thou kind even as Allah hath been kind to thee, and seek not corruption in the earth. Lo, Allah loveth not corrupters.* (Quran 28: 77)

*Wrong not mankind in their goods, and do not evil, making mischief in the earth.* (Quran 26: 183)

*Repel not those who call upon their Lord at morn and evening, seeking His Countenance. Thou art not accountable for them in aught, nor are they accountable for thee in aught that thou shouldst repel them and be of the wrong-doers.* (Quran 6: 52)

*The way of blame is only against those who oppress mankind, and wrongfully rebel in the earth. For such there is a painful doom.* (Quran 42:42)

*O ye messengers! Eat of good things and do right. Lo I am aware of what you do. And lo, this your religion is one religion and I am your Lord, so keep your duty unto Me. But the mankind have broken their religion amongst them into sects, each sect rejoicing its tenants.* (Quran 23: 51-53)

*This day are all good things made lawful for you. The food of those who have received the Scriptures is lawful for you, and your food is lawful for them. And so are the virtuous women of the believers and virtuous women of those who received the Scripture before you lawful for you. When ye give them their marriage portions and live with them in honor, not in fornication, nor taking them as secret concubines. Who denieth the faith, his work is vain and he will be among the losers in the Hereafter.* (Quran 5: 5)

*Establish worship, pay the poor due, and bow your heads with those who bow in worship. Enjoin ye righteousness upon mankind while ye yourselves forget to practice it? And ye are readers of the Scriptures! Have you no sense?* (Quran 2:43-44)

*Confound not truth with falsehood, nor knowingly conceal the truth.* (Quran 2:42)

*As for those who sunder their religion and become schismatic, no concern at all thou hast with them. Their case will go to Allah, who then will tell them what they used to do.* (Quran 6: 160)

*Those who spend of which Allah hath given them in ease and in adversity, those who control their wrath and are forgiving toward mankind. Allah loveth the good.* (Quran 3: 134)

*And they have broken their religion into fragments amongst them, yet all are returning to Us.* (Quran 21: 93)

*Before long, Allah will bring friendly relations between you and those whom you regard as your enemies. And Allah is Powerful, and Allah is Forgiving, Merciful.* (Quran 60: 7)

*And for every nation have We appointed a ritual, that they may mention the name of Allah on the beast of cattle; and your God is one God, therefore surrender unto Him. And give good tidings, O Muhammad, to the humble.* (Quran 22: 34)

*Revile not those unto whom they pray beside Allah lest they wrongfully revile Allah through ignorance. Thus unto every nation have We made their deed seem fair. Then unto their Lord is their return, and He will tell them what they used to do!* (Quran 6: 109)

Abu Hanifa and Abu Yusuf say, "Liquor produced by means of wheat, barley, honey or millet is lawful, provided it not be drunk in a wanton manner, quoting Prophet Muhammad from Hadith: Khamr— wine is the product of these two trees, the vine and the date palm."

*Say unto the people of the Scripture: dispute ye with us concerning Allah when He is our Lord and your Lord? Ours are our works and yours your works. We look to Him alone.* (Quran 2: 139)

*There shall be no sin imputed unto those who believe and do good works for what they may have eaten. So be mindful of your duty to Allah and do good works, and again be mindful of your duty and believe, and once again be mindful of your duty and do right. Allah loveth the good.* (Quran 5: 93)

*O ye who believe! Let not a folk deride a folk who may be better than they are, nor let women deride who may be better than they are; neither defame one another, nor insult one another by nicknames. Bad is the name of lewdness after faith. And whoso turneth not in repentance, such are evil-doers.* (Quran 49:9)

*O ye who believe. Obey Allah and obey the Messenger and those of you who are in authority, and if ye have a dispute concerning any matter, refer it to Allah and the Messenger if ye are in truth believers in Allah and the Last Day. That is better and most seemly in the end.* (Quran 4:19)

*As for those who believe in Allah, and hold fast unto Him, them He will cause to enter into His mercy and grace, and will guide them unto Him by a straight road.* (Quran 4:176)

*Alif Lam Mim. Ra. These are verses of the Scripture. That which is revealed unto thee from thy Lord is the Truth, but most of mankind believe not.* (Quran 13:1)

*He it is Who showeth you the lightning, a fear and a hope, and raiseth the heavy clouds.* (Quran 13:12)

*The thunder hymneth His praise and so do the angels in awe of Him. He launcheth the thunderbolts and smiteth with them whom He will while they dispute in doubt concerning Allah, and He is mighty in wrath.* (Quran 13:13)

*Unto Him is the real prayer. Those unto whom they pray beside Allah respond to them not at all, save as is the response to one who stretcheth forth his hands toward water asking that it may come into his mouth and it will never reach it. The prayer of disbeliever goeth far astray.* (Quran 13:14)

*With clear proofs and writings: and We have revealed unto thee the Remembrance that thou mayest explain to mankind that which hath been revealed for them, and that haply they may reflect.* (Quran 16:44)

*Lo this Quran guideth unto that which is straightest, and giveth tiding unto the believers who do good works that theirs will be a great reward.* (Quran 17:9)

*Lo, those who distort Our revelations are not hid from Us. Is he who is hurled into Fire better, or he who cometh secure on the Day of Resurrection? Do what ye will. Lo, He is seer of what ye do.* (Quran 41: 40)

*Whoso doeth right it is for his soul, and whoso doeth wrong it is against it. And thy Lord is not all tyrant to His slaves.* (Quran 41: 46)

*Whosoever goeth right, it is only for the good of his own soul that he goeth right, and whosoever erreth, erreth only to its hurt. No laden soul can bear another's load. We never punish until We have sent a messenger.* (Quran 17: 15)

*And no burdened soul can bear another's burden, and if one heavy laden crieth for help with his load, naught of it will be lifted even though unto whom he crieth be of kin. Thou warnest only those who fear their Lord in secret, and have established worship. He who groweth in goodness groweth only for himself, he cannot by his merit redeem others. Unto Allah is the journeying.* (Quran 35: 18)

*The blind man is not equal with the seer. Nor is darkness tantamount to light. Nor is the shadow equal with sun's heat. Nor are the living equal with the dead. Lo, Allah maketh whom He will to hear. Thou canst not reach those who are in the graves. Thou art but a warner. Lo, we have sent thee with the Truth, a bearer of glad tidings and a warner. And there is not a nation but a warner hath passed among them.* (Quran 35: 19-24)

*And if they deny thee, those before them also denied. Their messengers came unto them with clear proofs of Allah's sovereignty and with the Psalms and the Scripture giving light.* (Quran 35: 25)

*If ye are thankless, yet Allah is Independent of you. Though He is not pleased with the thanklessness for his bondmen, and if ye are thankful He is pleased therewith with you. No laden soul will bear another's load. Then unto your Lord is your return, and He will tell you what ye used to do. Lo, He knoweth what is in the breasts of men.* (Quran 39: 7)

*And they who believe and whose seed follow them in faith, We cause their seed to join them there, and We deprive them of naught of their life's work. Every man is a pledge for that which he has earned.* (Quran 52: 21)

*Every soul is a pledge for its own deeds.* (Quran 74: 38)

*Almost might the heavens above be rent asunder while the angels hymn the praise of their Lord and ask forgiveness for those on the earth. Lo, Allah is the Forgiver, the Merciful.* (Quran 42: 5)

*Liken they then to Allah that which is bred up in outward show, and in dispute cannot make itself plain.* (Quran 43:18)

*For each period is a Book. God annuls or confirms what He pleases. For with Him is the Mother of the Book. Whether we shall show you while you are living: Some of what we promised them or take your soul to Ourselves before it is fulfilled, your duty is only to convey the Message. Ours is the reckoning.* (Quran 13:39-40)

*For when we assigned to Abraham the site of the Temple. We said to him: Do not attribute divinity to anything beside Me. And purify My Temple for those who will walk around it, and those who will stand before it. And those who will bow down in prostration. And so, proclaim the pilgrimage to all people: They will come to you on foot and on every kind of fast conveyance, coming from every far-away place, so that they might experience much that shall be of benefit to them, and they might glorify God's name.* (Quran 22:26-28)

*And your creation or your resurrection is in no other way than a single soul: for God is He Who Hears and Sees all things.* (Quran 31:28)

*Whatever you are given here is for the convenience of this life, but that which is with God is better and more enduring. For those who have faith and put their trust in their Sustainer, those who avoid the greater crimes and shameful deeds and when they are angry, even then forgive. Those who pay attention to their Instructor and are constant in prayer. Who conduct their affairs by mutual consultation and who give out of the sustenance We bestow on them.* (Quran 42: 36-38)

*So I call to witness the rosy glow of sunset, the night and its progression. And the moon as it grows in fullness. Surely, you shall travel from stage to stage. What then is the matter with them that they do not have faith in the unfolding?* (Quran 84: 16-20)

The statement of Allah: Show forgiveness, enjoin what is good, and turn away from the foolish, don't punish them. Al Bukhari [V.7:199]

Allah ordered His Prophet to forgive the people their misbehavior toward him. Al Bukhari [6:167-O.B]

During the life of the Prophet, paying zakat was not a universal requirement for becoming a Muslim, and that the Prophet accepted conversion to Islam even with the stipulation of non-payment. Abdullahi Ahmed An-Na'Im

## Wisdom of the Prophet

The Prophet said, "If the devotion of the two Muslims is in their swords, both the killer and the killed are in for the Fire."

When the Prophet sent two representatives to govern Yemen, he told them, "Bring ease, not hardship. Bring good news, not horror. And cooperate willingly with each other."

When the Christian king of Ethiopia died, the Prophet said to his people, "A righteous man has died today, so stand up and pray for your brother."

Abu Hurairah relates, "The Messenger of God was asked who are the most noble of people?"

He said, "The most conscientious of them."

They said, "This is not what we are asking you about."

He said, "Then it would be Joseph, a prophet of God who was a son of the prophet of God, who was a son of Abraham, the Friend of God."

They said, "This is not what we are asking you about."

He said, "Then you are asking me about the original nobility of the Arabs. The best of them in ignorance are the best of them in Islam when they have come to understanding."

The Prophet Muhammad's sayings were recorded by many writers during his lifetime, including women writers. Most of the traditions of the Prophet collected during the Umayyad period either perished or were incorporated into the literature of the Abbasid period. The subjects covered during those periods were divided into two categories, religious and non-religious. The non-religious subjects comprised poetry, proverbs, medicine, genealogy, mineralogy and the pre-Islamic history. In the category of the religious subjects were the Quran, commentary on the Quran, collection of the Hadiths, books on the acts of worship. Books on inheritance and other topics of law. Books on zakat and taxation. Biography of the Prophet and the early history of the Caliphs.

Later authors studying the lives of the Caliphs during the Umayyad period wrote mostly about the current traditions of the Muslims. One author by the name of Goldziher noted that the Umayyad Caliphs were hardly concerned with the law but rather with ethics, asceticism, eschatology and the politics. He observed that the Muslim community was quite ignorant of the Islamic traditions as dogma or religious practices. They were unable to incorporate their customs within a systematic ideology. His most candid of observations was that Muslims were fighting in the name of Islam and even built mosques, yet in Syria they did not know that only five prayers a day were obligatory, and for this knowledge they had to refer to an old Companion of the Prophet. Thus in literal sense of the word, Sharia didn't exist during the reign of the early and later Caliphs in succession.

During the lifetime of the Prophet, his sayings were considered the law of the land, which if heeded in perfect spirit of Islamic virtues, it could be rightfully defined as Sharia in its pure essence of exemplary living. 'Islam in Society' published Prophet's sayings in series of Units for Muslim students to study and contemplate. Only a handful of his sayings are cited below, neglected by historians, sidelining Prophet's light of love and justice with onerous human interpretations in stark contrast to his message of peace and harmony.

The Quran is revealed with five categories. Things lawful, things unlawful, clear and positive teachings, stories, and allegories. So hold lawful what is lawful for you and hold forbidden the things which are forbidden. Act according to the clear teachings. Draw moral benefits from the stories and affirm faith in the allegories.

Those who are nearest to Allah are those who are the first to give a greeting.

He who believes in Allah and the Last Day should honor his guests with love and courtesy.

Allah commands us to address the elderly with kindness. Don't say to them a word of anger, nor repel them, always treat them honorably.

Allah indeed has forbidden you to disobey your parents.

Remember the revelations. History is a witness. Certainly humanity is truly lost. Except those who have faith, practice righteousness, and who teach each other truth and perseverance.

Allah has divided mercy into a hundred parts, out of which he retains ninety-nine parts with Him, and has sent the one remaining to earth. From this one part emanates all the compassion that the whole of creations shows towards each other. So much so that an animal will lift her hoof above her young lest it should get hurt.

# Chapter 7 ~ Sharia Unlidded

*And We have sent thee Muhammad only as a bearer of good tidings and a warner.* (Quran 25: 56)

According to general belief, ahadith was orally transmitted at least for one hundred years. Al Zuhri was the first one who recorded them. On the authenticity of this statement, there are differences of opinion among orientalists. Muir accepts it with the remark that there are no authentic remains of any such compilation of an earlier date than the middle of second century of Hijra. While Guillaume states, Hadith must be regarded as an invention.

The official influence and activity in the fabrication of Hadith goes back to a very early period. The alleged instructions given by Muayiya to Al Mughira to denounce Ali and his followers, to drive them away and not listen to them as a source of ahadith, always praise Uthman and his followers, to have close contact with them, and to listen to them as a source of ahadith, was an official statement to encourage the production and diffusion of ahadith hostile to Ali and in favor of Uthman.

The first fabrication of traditions began in the political sphere, crediting and discrediting the parties concerned. In the well-known work of Al Shaukani concerning spurious and similar traditions approximate numbers are agreed upon by the scholars.

Forty-two spurious traditions about the Prophet

Thirty-eight spurious traditions about the first three caliphs

Ninety-six spurious traditions about Ali and his wife Fatima

Fourteen spurious traditions about Muayiya

> Therefore, it looks as if the spurious traditions began to originate for political purposes at and about the period of war between Ali and Muayiya, and continued later on as a counter attack on the Umayyad dynasty. The traditionalists and other scholars found it necessary from that time onwards to be more cautious in selecting their authorities (M. Mustafa Azmi).

The systemic development of Sharia began during the early Abbasid era, after Year 750. The view of the relatively late evolution of Sharia as a coherent and self-contained system in Islamic history is clear from the time frame for the emergence of major schools of thought, the systematic collection of Sunna as the second and more detailed source of Sharia, and the development of the judicial methodology. All these developments took place in the second and third centuries of Islam. The early Abbasid era witnessed the emergence of the main schools of Islamic jurisprudence, including those still known today.

The surviving schools are attributed to Jafar al-Sadiq, the founder of the main school of Shia jurisprudence, he died in Year 765. Abu Hanifa died Year 767, Maliki died Year 795, Al Shafi died Year 820 and Hanbal died Year 855. Al Shafi is commonly acknowledged to have laid the foundation of Usul al-fiqh to regulate the interpretation of the Quran and the Sunna, but the process of collection and authentication of Sunna reports continued beyond his time. The most authoritative compilation of Sunna for Sunni Muslims are attributed to Al Bukhari who died Year 870 and death in succession of other theologian, Muslim Year 875, Ibn Majah Year 886, Abu Dawud Year 888, al Tirmidhi Year 892, al Nasa Year 915. For Shia, the most authoritative compilations also emerged during that general time frame, namely those attributed to al Kulayni Year 941, Ibn Bahawayh Year 991, al Tusi Year 1067. The subsequent development and spread of various schools have been influenced by many social, political and demographic factors, which have sometimes resulted in shifting schools from one region to another, thus confining them to certain parts as is the case with Shia schools at present.

Fiqh and Sharia are the products of human interpretation of the Quran and Sunnah of the Prophet in a particular historical context. Whether a given proposition is said to be based on Fiqh or Sharia, it is subject to the risks of same human error, ideological or political bias, or influence by its proponents' economic interests and social concerns.

> Once the centrality of the human agency is recognized, whether in the interpretation of the Sharia or in general social change, many creative possibilities of reform and transformation will emerge. Times of severe crisis as experienced by Islamic societies and communities today should lead Muslims to question prevalent assumptions and challenge existing

insinuations that have failed to deliver on the promise of liberation and development (Abdullahi Ahmed An-Na'Im).

As related by Ahmad and Abu Dawud in Fiqh-us Sunnah, "When a person comes to the mosque, he should look at his shoes. If he finds any filth on them, he should wipe them against the ground and pray in them."

Aisha related that the Messenger of Allah kissed her while he was fasting and said, "Kissing does not nullify the ablution, nor does it break the fast." Related by Ishaq and Bazzar in Fiqh-us-Sunnah.

> The Prophet Muhammad said, "Fasting is not abstaining from eating and drinking only, but also from vain speech and foul language. If one of you is being cursed or annoyed, he should say, I am fasting, I am fasting" (Fiqh-us-Sunnah).

> "There is no negligence in sleep, but negligence occurs when one is awake. If one of you forgets a prayer or sleeps through its time, then he should pray it when he remembers" (Prophet Muhammad Fiqh-us-Sunnah).

In view of the Prophet's saying above, most scholars agree that one can make up missed prayers after the morning and afternoon prayers.

> "Under certain circumstances, one is allowed to combine two prayers together since the Prophet said he didn't want any hardships for his Ummah" (Fiqh-us-Sunnah).

> "Aisha became the first woman Imam to lead the women in prayer, then Umm Salmah" (Fiqh-us-Sunnah).

> "Women participated in discussions with the Prophet and his companions. Caliph Omar appointed a slave woman to lead the women of his family in prayers during the nights of Ramadan" (Safia Iqbal).

**Light Prayer of the Prophet:**

O Allah make light in my heart, and light in my vision and light in my hearing and light on my right and light behind me and light in my nerves and light in my flesh and light in my hair and light in my skin (Fiqh-us-Sunnah).

## Rain Prayer of the Prophet:

All praise is due to Allah, the Gracious, the Merciful, the king of the Day of Judgment. There is no God but Allah Who does what he wishes. O Allah there is no God except Thee. You are the Self-sufficient and we are the poor. Send down rain upon us and make it a source of strength for us and satisfaction for us (Fiiqh-us-Sunnah).

## Poetry of Islam:

Extremists in different parts of the world and at different times have portrayed the music and poetry as evil, dogmatically and erroneously, going as far as banning music and burning musical instruments. Empowered with zeal to shut down the music shops and forbidding the recitation of poetry, they remain steeped deep inside the murky waters of ignorance. There is not a single verse in the Quran forbidding music or recitation of poetry. Traditions of the Prophet encourage poets to share and perfect their talents.

*God hath treasuries beneath the Throne, the keys whereof are the tongues of poets; he who knows his own self knows God.* Prophet Muhammad

The Quran is a treasure-trove of poetry and its recitation music to the ears of the believers. God's creation, too, is a medley of musical notes in rhythm with the universal song of love and beauty. Air is the flute in the sky, thunder the drums, and lightning the harp of universal melody. The trees sing and whisper against the frolicking breeze and the entire cosmos quivers with ecstasy at the very sound of song and music in nature played over the strings of the luminaries. The Hadith itself validates that the Prophet Muhammad was moved to ecstasy by the recitation of the poetry. One evening the Prophet was sitting in his mosque in Medina with his followers, answering questions and interpreting the revelations, and chose to recite this verse below.

*He is the One Who caused the Book to descend upon you. Part of it is clearly defined, verses, which are 'mother of the Book', and others are symbolic. But those with error in their hearts follow the symbolic part of it, seeking dissention and seeking its interpretation. None knows its interpretation except Allah, and those who are firmly rooted in knowledge. Others say, we have faith in it, it is all from our Lord. But none recalls except those who possess the inner Heart.* (Quran 3: 7)

After he had recited this verse, a poet by the name of Kaab ibn Salma sang this impromptu poem to compliment the revelation the prophet had just recited.

Love like a venomous snake has tormented my heart
But for this illness there is neither physician, nor sorcerer
Only my Beloved
With Whom I am so much in love
Can cure me
For He possesses the medicines and incantations
For my malady.

The Prophet Muhammad's soul was moved to ecstasy by the beauty of this poem, and he didn't even know that he had leapt to his feet in a state of mystical abandon. He seemed oblivious to all, his face revealing the deep-hearted mystery of his own self, where Allah was the Beloved and he the Lover, with a longing pure and sublime to be united with the Beloved. The Prophet's right hand shot upward, palm toward the heavens as if receiving blessings from the blessed Beloved. His left hand, palm down, was poised toward the earth, as if bestowing the blessed gift of blessings upon the world. With the grace of a skilful dancer, he had begun to spin on his toes, his black cloak slipping from his shoulders, and falling to the ground in one undulating heap.

*You are of me, Ali, and I am of you!* The Prophet's voice was in tune with the rhythm of his body, whirling and floating. *Come, dance with me, and learn the art of receiving with your right hand divine blessings and inspiration from Allah—the Beloved, and bestowing them with your left hand upon all creatures of the world.*

Ali was quick to bounce to his feet, joining the Prophet Muhammad. Swift and ecstatic were Ali's movements, his toes were spinning in unison with Muhammad's, and his soul sailing aloft to heights unattainable. The Prophet's lips were pouring another song, urging Ali's brother Jafar to taste the sweetness of this cosmic mystery.

*Come, Jafar, join us. You are like me in both looks and character.* The Prophet Muhammad was inviting all to participate in this cosmic dance of love and self-surrender.

Aflame by the torch of divine love, the bodies of these three men were floating and swirling! They were spinning on their toes in unison as if attracted together to the centre of the earth, their bodies whirling like the sparkling atoms to be consumed by the light of the sun. This cosmic dance on the very rungs of culmination had come to a sudden halt, enveloping the three participants in the light of bliss and rapture. The Prophet Muhammad had retrieved his cloak, and stood splitting it into rags.

*This is the dance of Oneness.* The Prophet Muhammad scattered the pieces of his black cloak over the heads of his congregation. *My cousins are like the stars, whichever one of them you follow, they will guide you.*

*Was that enjoyable, Prophet?* Omar ibn Khattab asked, more aghast than awed, oblivious to the rapt expression of his wife Zainab and their daughter Hafsa.

*For sure, Omar! When Beloved calls, the Lover can't help but be consumed by the fire of joy and ecstasy.* Prophet Muhammad's pomegranate-red lips were spilling the fire of rubies. *Allah, the Beloved is inside the hearts of all human beings, but love is the key to unlock the spiritual heart to see one's Beloved. Love, ecstasy and oblivion are the prerequisites to meet our one and only Beloved, through the fire of longing, after we have reduced our ego to ashes and after our mortal attributes of wisdom are effaced.*

Later Kaab recited more poems, one of those was about the she-camel who bore his mistress away.

Her eyes like those of the lonely white Oryx, gazed across the stony wilderness

Her neck was heavy, her forehead high as a millstone, her flanks robust

Male-like, full in the cheek, no tick ever penetrated her hide

Foaled by a noble dam, long-necked, smooth breasted and nimble

Well-bred with her eagle nose, heavy ears, muzzle like a pick-ax

Sira, the traditional book for the Prophet's biographies records several poets who stayed with the Prophet at Medina and wrote for him and about him. Ibn Ishaq, one of the Prophet's biographer wrote volumes of poetry. One of the Medinese poet by the name of Ansari Hassan likens the Prophet to light in his poem below:

Amongst us stands the Prophet, a shooting star followed

By light, outstripping all shooting stars
Truth is his speech, justice his way of life
Whoso answers his call is saved from destruction
Another of Hassan's poem weaves banners of his own tribe with
those of the Prophet.
God honored us through the victory of His Prophet
With us He built the pillars of Islam
Through us He brought glory to His Prophet and His Book
Us He glorified with fighting and courage
Gabriel visits our dwellings
Reading Islam's laws and duties
Kab ibn Zubayr also calls Prophet light in his poem:
The Prophet is a light, illuminating the way to truth
An Indian blade unsheathed from the blades of God
Amidst a band from Quraysh one of whom had said to them
In the center of Mecca, Be Gone, when they embraced Islam
They went, but did not retreat like weak men without armor
When battle raged, or like men unsteady in the saddle untrained
Haughty-nosed are they, heroes, wielding shields, decked in
armor
They do not rejoice when their spears give them victory over a
people
Nor do they panic if they are beaten
Their battle wounds are suffered only from the front
They tarry not from the pools of death
Even after the death of the Prophet Muhammad, poets found
patronage from a succession of Caliphs. Abu Aswad al-Duaali
Year 688 was a famous poet, proclaiming the love of Prophet, Ali
and his family as essential to faith and salvation.
I love Muhammad with a passionate love
As I do Abbas, Hamza and the Wasiyy
I love them through love of God so that
I present myself, when resurrected, impeccable
A love I was bequeathed ever since
The windmills of Islam turned, a love unequalled
The sarcastic men of the tribe of Quraysh say to me

Do not ever forget, Ali
Sons of the Prophet's uncle and his kin
These are of all mankind my greatest loves
If love of them is rational, I hit the mark
If irrational, I do not thereby sin

The Poets kept singing the praises of the Prophet Muhammad centuries after his death. The most famous Egyptian poet, Muhammad ibn Said al-Busiri Year 1296 follows the theme of love for the Prophet:

He is the beloved, whose intercession is hoped for
From every horror one is plunged in
Like the sun that appears small from afar
But blunts the eye when closely beheld
His majesty is such that be, a single man
Appears when you approach him, as though
Amidst an army and courtiers

Grant me leave to describe his wonders that appeared
Like the fires of hospitality even by night on mountain-tops
Pearls gain in beauty when strung together
But lose none of their esteem when single
Its verses contain meanings like waves in their profusion
But superior to them in beauty and value
Countless their wonders and numberless
No matter how often recited, never fatiguing

I waited upon him with a hymn of praise, seeking to be rid
Of the sins of a lifetime of poetry and waiting upon others
For sins had garlanded me with fearful consequences
And I appeared like the animals garlanded for sacrifice
I obeyed the temptations of youth in both my callings
Reaping nothing but wickedness and regret
What a loss my soul suffered in its commerce
It failed to exchange this world for the next, it failed even to bargain

But if I commit a sin, my allegiance at least is not severed
To the Prophet, nor is my rope cut away
Far be it from him to deny his favors to one who seeks him
Or turn away in disgrace one who desires his shelter
Another Egyptian poet Ahmad Shawqi between years 1868-1932
begins with an amatory prelude.
A white antelope, standing on the plain between willow and
mountain
Sanctioned the shedding of my blood, in sacred months
Fate struck a lion with the eyes of a doe
O denizens of the plains, hurry to aid the denizen of the den

Though my sins may be too grave to forgive, yet a hope I cherish
Before God, places me with the best of protectors
When I lower the wing of humility I shall ask him
For grace of his intercession and little do I ask
I cling to the gate of the Prince of the Prophets, and whoso
Holds the key to God's gate must prosper
Muhammad chosen of God and His mercy
The object of God's desire, of spirits and creatures

When Bahira saw him he said: We recognize him
From what we have learnt of names and signs
Granting him shade, and deriving shade from him
Was a cloud humped be the best of rain showers
It was the love of a Messenger of God instilled in the hearts
Of men recluse in monasteries and hermits on mountaintops

They say: You conquered, but the Messengers of God were not
sent
To kill souls, nor did they come to shed blood
This is ignorance, misrepresentation, sophistry
You conquered with the sword after you had conquered with
the pen
Exile confronted with good, renders one incapable

Of checking it, but confronted with evil it recedes
Had Christianity not had its protectors, brandishing their swords
It would not have benefited from its mercy and clemency
It is the adherents of Jesus who have now readied all instruments of war
And we have readied nothing but a state of weakness

The Sura eleventh in the Quran tells of other prophets of Arabia not mentioned in the Hebrew Scripture. This Sura is named Hud after an Arab prophet from the tribe of Aad. More prophets of Arabia are recorded in Hadith, that of Salih of the tribe of Thamud and Shueyb of the Midian, identified with Jethro, which, with those of Noah and Moses.

*And unto the tribe of Aad We sent their brother Hud. He said: O my people, serve Allah! Ye have no other God save Him. Lo, ye do but invent.* (Quran 11: 50)

Dhikr—Remembrance of God:

*O ye who believe! Celebrate the praise of Allah and do so often. And glorify him morning and evening.* (Quran 33:41-42)

Narrated Abu Musa that the Prophet said to him: O Abu Musa, you have been given one of the musical wind instruments of the family of David (6:568-O.B.)

Allah says: I am to my servant as he expects of Me. I am with him when he remembers Me. If he remembers Me in his heart I remember him to Myself and if he remembers Me in an assembly, I mention him in an assembly better than his, and if he draws near to Me a hand's span, I draw nearer to him an arm's length, and if he draws near to Me an arm's length, I draw nearer to him a fathom length, and if he comes to Me walking, I run to him at great speed (Al Bukhari 9:502-O.B.).

*Lo, those who believe this Revelation and those who are the Jews and the Sabaeans and the Christians and the Magians and the idolaters. Lo, Allah will decide between them on the Day of Resurrection. Lo, Allah is witness over all things.* (Quran 22: 17)

*O ye who believe, draw not near unto prayer when ye are drunken, till ye know that which ye utter, nor when you are polluted, save when journeying upon the road, till ye have bathed. And if ye be ill, or on a journey, or one of you cometh from the closet, or ye have touched women, and ye find not water, then go to high clean soil and rub your faces and your hands therewith. Lo, Allah is Benign, Forgiving.* (Quran 4:43)

Zakat: This term is derived from the Arabic Verbal root, meaning, to bless, to purify and to increase.

*Of their wealth take alms, so that thou mightiest purify and sanctify them.* Quran 9:103)

> The Prophet himself consistently referred to the Quran as a source of authority and only in the latter years in Medina did he refer to his own teachings and example—Sunnah as a guide to right conduct. The word Sharia and human interpretation of Law do not occur in Sunnah in their usual meanings. As is related in one of the Hadiths that when the Prophet was sending Muadh to the Yemen as ruler and judge, he was asked three questions as to what he would refer to when making decisions in his capacity as a judge? Muadh mentioned firstly the Quran, then the Sunnah of the Prophet and then his own exercise of judgment on the basis of Quran and Sunnah. There was no reference of Sharia in this Hadith, nor to any human interpretation of the Law. The word Sharia does not seem to have been used by any of the Caliphs after the demise of the Prophet, nor have they used its equivalent human interpretation of the Law in the sense of a legal code. These terminologies emerged much later and consist mainly of juristic designations that found currency when a body of juristic doctrine was developed over a period of time. There is no historical precedent to support the suggestion that the Sharia cannot be revitalized. The process of its interpretation in the early days of Islam documented that it is not a fixed and permanent entity but capable of change to fit new circumstances (Mohammad Hashim Kamali).

# Chapter 8 ~ Sharia for Peace

*These are the portents of Allah which we recite unto thee Muhammad with truth, and lo, thou art of the number of our messengers.* (Quran 2: 252)

If Muslims wish to govern by the Law of Sharia, they should heed the Messenger of Allah, living in conformity with the true precepts of Islam in all its purity of peace, justice and equality. The Prophet Muhammad's Sharia, if it is to be called Sharia based on the example of his life and the Quranic injunctions, is not about rituals, punishment, jurisprudence, but about love, unity and forgiveness. He envisioned and practiced Islam as the religion of peace and reconciliation.

*And O Muhammad say: My Lord! Forgive and have mercy, for Thou art best of all who show mercy.* (Quran 23:118)

*Had it not been for the grace of Allah and His mercy unto you, and that Allah is Clement, Merciful, ye had been undone.* (Quran 24: 20)

*And lo, thy Lord! He is indeed the Mighty, the Merciful.* (Quran 26: 9)

*Announce O Muhammad unto my slaves that verily I am the Merciful, the Forgiving.* (Quran 15: 49)

*Know they not that Allah is He Who accepteth repentance from his bondmen and taketh the alms, and that Allah is He Who is the Merciful, the Relenting.* (Quran 9: 104)

*For them is the abode of peace with their Lord. He will be their Protecting Friend because of what they used to do.* (Quran 6: 128)

*Confound not truth with falsehood, nor knowingly conceal the truth.* (Quran 2: 42)

*He hath revealed unto thee Muhammad the Scripture with truth, confirming that which was revealed before it, even as He revealed the Torah and the Gospel.* (Quran 3: 3)

*Say O Muhammad to mankind: If you love Allah, follow me. Allah will love you and forgive your sins. Allah is Merciful, Forgiving.* (Quran 3: 31)

*And let not those who possess ease and dignity among you swear not to give to the near of kin and to the needy, and to fugitives for the cause of Allah. Let them forgive and show indulgence. Yearn ye not that Allah may forgive you? Allah is Merciful, Forgiving.* (Quran 24: 22)

*Save him who repenteth and believeth and doth righteous work, as for such, Allah will change their evil deeds to good deeds. Allah is ever Merciful, Forgiving.* (Quran 25: 70)

*Enjoin ye righteousness upon mankind, while ye yourselves forget to practice it. And ye are the readers of Scripture! Have ye then no sense?* (Quran 2: 44)

*A kind word with forgiveness is better than almsgiving followed by injury. Allah is Absolute, Clement.* (Quran 2: 263)

*He knoweth that which goes down into the earth and that which cometh from it, and that which descendeth from the heaven and that which ascendeth into it. He is the Merciful, the Forgiving.* (Quran 34: 2)

*And make mention O Muhammad in the Scripture of Abraham. Lo, he was a saint, a Prophet.* (Quran 19: 41)

*Wherein are plain materials for Allah's guidance the place where Abraham stood up to pray, and whosoever entereth it is safe. And pilgrimage to the House is a duty unto Allah for mankind, for him who can find a way thither. As for him who disbelieveth, let him know that, lo, Allah is Independent of all creatures.* (Quran 3: 97)

*And make mention in the Scripture of Ishmael. Lo, he was a keeper of his promise, and he was a messenger of Allah, a Prophet.* (Quran 19: 54)

*He enjoined upon his people worship and almsgiving and he was acceptable in the sight of his Lord.* (Quran 19: 55)

*And make mention in the Scripture of Idris (Enoch). Lo, he was a saint, a Prophet.* (Quran 19: 56)

*And make mention of Ishmael and Elisha and Dhul-Kifl. All are of the chosen.* (Quran 38: 49)

*This is a reminder. And lo, for all those who ward off evil is a happy journey's end.* (Quran 38: 50)

*And verily We gave unto Moses the Scripture and We caused a train of messengers to follow him, and We gave unto Jesus, son of Mary, clear proofs of Allah's sovereignty and We supported him with the Holy Spirit. Is it ever so, that, when there cometh unto you a messenger from Allah, with that which ye yourself desire not, ye grow arrogant and some ye disbelieve and some ye slay?* (Quran 2: 87)

*Say unto the people of Scripture: Dispute ye with us concerning Allah when He is our Lord and your Lord. Ours are our works and yours your works. We look to Him alone.* (Quran 2: 139)

*When you are greeted with a greeting, greet ye with a better than it or return it. Lo, Allah taketh account of all things.* (Quran 4: 86)

*Degrees of rank from Him, and forgiveness and mercy. Allah is ever Merciful, Forgiving.* (Quran 4: 96)

*As for such, it may be that Allah will pardon them. Allah is ever Clement, Forgiving.* (Quran 4: 99)

*Yet whoso doeth evil, or wrongeth his own soul, then seeketh pardon of Allah, will find Allah Merciful, Forgiving.* (Quran 4: 110)

*O children of Adam! Look to your adornment at every place of worship, and eat and drink, but be not prodigal. Lo, he loveth not the prodigals.* (Quran 7: 31)

*If you do good openly or keep it secret, or forgive evil? Lo, Allah is Powerful, Forgiving.* (Quran 4: 149)

*But those who believe in Allah and His messengers and make no distinction between any of them, unto them Allah will give their wages, and Allah is ever Merciful, Forgiving.* (Quran 4: 151)

*Lo, my Protecting Friend is Allah who revealeth the Scripture. He befriendeth the righteous.* (Quran 7: 196)

*Keep to forgiveness O Muhammad, and enjoin kindness, and turn away from the ignorant.* (Quran 7: 199)

*Know they not that Allah is He Who accepteth penance from His bondsmen and taketh the alms, and that Allah is He Who is the Merciful, the Relenting.* (Quran 9: 104)

*Ask pardon of your Lord and then turn unto him in repentance. Lo, my Lord is Loving, Merciful.* (Quran 11: 90)

*Announce O Muhammad unto My slaves that verily I am the Merciful, the Forgiving.* (Quran 15: 49)

*And if you would count the favor of Allah ye cannot reckon it. Lo Allah is indeed Merciful, Forgiving.* (Quran 16: 18)

*Say: O My slaves who have been prodigal to their own hurt. Despair not of the mercy of Allah, Who forgiveth all sins. Lo, He is the Merciful, the Forgiving.* (Quran 39: 53)

*The seven heavens and the earth and all that is therein praise Him, and there is not a thing but hymneth His praise, but ye understand not their praise. Lo, He is ever Clement, Forgiving.* (Quran 17: 44)

*And we prescribed for them therein: The life for the life, and eye for the eye, and the nose for the nose, and the ear for the ear, and the tooth for the tooth, and for wounds retaliation. But whoso forgoeth it in the way of charity, it shall be expiation for him. Whoso judgeth not by that which Allah hath revealed, such are wrong-doers.* (Quran 5: 45)

*Will they not rather turn unto Allah and seek forgiveness of Him? For Allah is Merciful, Forgiving.* (Quran 5: 74)

*Then lo, thy Lord—for those who do evil in ignorance and afterward repent and amend. Lo, for them thy Lord is indeed Merciful, Forgiving.* (Quran 16: 119)

*And We caused Jesus, son of Mary, to follow in their footsteps, confirming that which was revealed before him, and We bestowed upon him the Gospel wherein is guidance and a light, confirming that which was revealed before it in the Torah—a guidance and admonition unto those who ward off evil.* (Quran 5: 46)

*When Allah saith: O Jesus, son of Mary! Remember My favor unto thee and unto thy mother, how I strengthened thee with the Holy Spirit, so that thou speakest unto mankind in the cradle as in maturity. And how I taught thee the Scripture and Wisdom and the Torah and the Gospel, and how thou didst shape of clay as if it were the likeness of a bird by My permission, and thou didst heal him who was born blind and the leper by My permission. And how thou didst raise the dead by My permission, and how I restrained the Children of Israel from harming thee when thou comest unto them with clear proofs, and those of them who disbelieved exclaimed: This is naught else than mere magic.* (Quran 5: 110)

*When the disciples said: O Jesus, son of Mary! Is thy Lord able to send down for us a table spread with food from heaven? He said: Observe your duty to Allah, if ye are true believes.* (Quran 5: 112)

*Jesus, son of Mary said: O Allah, Lord of us! Send down for us a table spread with food from heavens, that it may be a feast for us, for the first of us and for the last of us, and a sign from Thee. Give us sustenance, for Thou art the Best of Sustainers.* (Quran 5: 114)

*Allah said: Lo, I send it down for you. And whoso disbelieveth of you afterward, him surely I will punish with a punishment wherewith I have not punished any of My creatures.* (Quran 5: 115)

*And when Allah saith: O Jesus, son of Mary! Didst thou say unto mankind: Take me and my mother for two gods beside Allah? He saith: Be glorified! It was not mine to utter that to which I had no right. If I used to say it, then thou knowest it. Thou knowest what is in my mind, and I know not what is in Thy Mind. Lo, Thou, only Thou art the Knower of Things Hidden.* (Quran 5: 116)

*I spake unto them only that which Thou commandest me, saying: Worship Allah, my Lord and your Lord. I was a witness of them while I dwelt among them and when Thou tookest me Thou wast the Watcher over them. Thou art Witness over all things.* (Quran 5: 117)

*If Thou punish them, lo, they are Thy slaves, and if Thou forgive them, lo, they are Thy slaves. Lo, Thou only Thou art the Mighty, the Wise.* (Quran 5: 118)

*Allah saith: This is the day in which their truthfulness profiteth the truthful, for theirs are Gardens underneath which rivers flow, wherein they are secure forever, Allah taking pleasure in them and they in Him. That is the great triumph.* (Quran 5: 119)

*Unto Allah belongeth the Sovereignty of the heavens and the earth and whatsoever is therein, and He is able to do all things.* (Quran 5: 120)

*Then she brought him to her own folk, carrying him. They said: O Mary, thou hast come with an amazing thing.* (Quran 19: 27)

*O sister of Aaron! Thy father was not a wicked man, nor was thy mother a harlot.* (Quran 19: 28)

*Then she pointed to him. They said: How can we talk to one who is in the cradle, a young boy?* (Quran 19: 29)

*He spake! Lo, I am the slave of Allah. He hath given me the Scripture and hath appointed me a Prophet.* (Quran 19: 30)

*And hath made me blessed wheresoever I may be, and hath enjoined upon me prayer and alms-giving so long as I remain alive.* (Quran 19: 31)

*And hath made me dutiful toward her who bore me, and hath not made me unblest, arrogant.* (Quran 19: 32)

*Peace on me the day I was born, and the day I die, and the day I shall be raised alive.* (Quran 19: 33)

*Such was Jesus, son of Mary. This is a statement of the truth concerning which they doubt.* (Quran 19: 34)

*And she who was chaste, therefore, We breathed into her something of Our Spirit and made her and her son a token for all peoples.* (Quran 21: 91)

*And Mary, daughter of Imran, whose body was chaste, therefore we breathed therein something of Our Spirit. And she put faith in the words of her Lord and His Scriptures, and was of the obedient.* (Quran 66: 12)

*And when Jesus, son of Mary said: O Children of Israel! Lo, I am the messenger of Allah unto you, confirming that which was revealed before me in the Torah and bringing good tidings of a messenger who cometh after me, whose name is the Praised One! Yet when he hath come unto them with clear proofs, they say: This is mere magic.* (Quran 61: 6)

*And because of their saying: We slew the Messiah Jesus son of Mary. Allah's Messenger They slew him not, nor crucified, but it appeared unto them, and lo, those who disagree concerning it are in doubt thereof. They have no knowledge thereof save pursuit of conjecture, they slew him not for certain.* (Quran 4: 157)

*And when those who believe in Our revelations come unto thee, say: Peace be unto you! Your Lord hath prescribed for Himself mercy, that whoso of you doeth evil and repenteth afterward thereof and doth right, for him, lo, Allah is Merciful, Forgiving.* (Quran 6: 54)

*Such is the Knower of the visible and the invisible, the Mighty, the Merciful.* (Quran 32: 6)

*That Allah may reward the true men for their truth, or punish the hypocrites if He will, or relent toward them if He will. Lo, Allah is Merciful, Forgiving.* (Quran 33: 24)

*He it is who blesseth you and His angels bless you that He may bring you forth from darkness unto light, and He is Merciful to the believers.* (Quran 33: 43)

*And they say: Praise be to Allah who hath put grief away from us. Lo, our Lord is Forgiving, Bountiful.* (Quran 35: 34)

> It is necessary in social life to make mutual relations pleasant. The Holy Prophet has laid stress that to make mutual relations and to strengthen the bonds of society, it is necessary to speak out love for each other. So to achieve harmony and mutual peace (Hadith).

In the Bible it is said that first there was the Word, and there was Light. That means that the first or the highest knowledge is the truth. Light gives knowledge, words give knowledge. In fact, they are knowledge. The Quran says that Allah is the light of the heavens and the earth. That means the illumination to which one attains (Hazrat Inayat Khan).

# Chapter 9 ~ Sharia Recovered

*He is the knower of the visible and the invisible, the Great, the High
Exalted.* (Quran 13: 9)

No scholar is needed to recover Sharia from the wealth of the Quran.
Any Muslim without the taint of zeal can glean Laws of Islam from the
Quranic verses which would reveal the authentic precepts of Sharia,
beneficial not only to Muslims, but to all mankind. If Sharia could be
stripped clean of the connotation as the rendition of hateful laws which
have become the emblems of tyranny and oppression, of hate and
injustice, of brutal punishments and of savage treatment of women, it
could be polished with the gold of truth. It can then be implemented as
the universal measure of empathy, equality, compassion, tolerance, and
cultivating the virtues of peace, love and harmony. The verses below
are a part of the effort in designing the Code of Islamic Law which
Muslim States would be proud to practice, free of error and not
burdened by false teachings where warfare, violence, hatemongering,
and suppression of women is dreaded by the world. The world is
waiting for the Muslims to invent, reinvent, and re-write Sharia with
interpretations which are conducive to the image of Islam, not harmful
to its growth and acceptance.

The idea of all Muslims being a part of one community—the
Ummah—is basic to Islam. The Ummah was to live its life in accordance
with the same norms of patience, humility, generosity and mindfulness
as of the Prophet. It was to be motivated by the same desire—to be truly
obedient to Allah. Its scripture was the word of God, eternal and
unalterable, and it lay down the fundamental duties of every Muslim.
All Muslims are governed by the same laws. The Quran specifically
mentions Jews and Christians as People of the Book and they are free to
practice their religion under the governance of Islam. Muslim rulers
extended this rule to other religions based on the assertion of the Quran
that God sent prophets to all nations.

Hadith or tradition is the way the Sunnah was preserved after
Muhammad died. These traditions have forged a historical link

between Muslims and their Prophet. To prevent people from wrongfully attributing facts to him, a methodology was evolved to test the genuine from the spurious. The witnesses and a chain of authorities directly linking to the Prophet had to be provided to substantiate each Hadith before it was accepted.

This rule governing the Muslims' lives is called Sharia—the way. They cover all contingencies of human existence from birth to death and from an all-encompassing legal system.

> The need to determine Sharia law in detail led to the development of fiqh—human interpretation, the science of Islamic jurisprudence. Fiqh has four roots, the Quran, the Hadith, the Ijma—consensus amongst scholars—collective reasoning and Qayas—analogical deduction in individual reasoning (Azra Kidwai).

*A kind word with forgiveness is better than almsgiving followed by injury. Allah is Absolute, Clement.* (Quran 2: 263)

*My Lord! Lo, they have led many of mankind astray. But whoso followeth me, he verily is of me. And whoso disobeyeth me, still Thou art Merciful, Forgiving.* (Quran 14: 36)

*Establish worship at two ends of the day and in some watches of the night. Lo, good deeds annul ill deeds. This is a reminder for the mindful.* (Quran 11: 114)

*Seest thou not how Allah coineth a similitude: A goodly saying as a goodly tree, its root set firm, its branches reaching unto heaven.* (Quran 14: 24)

*Giving its fruit at every season by permission of its Lord. Allah coineth the similitudes for mankind in order that they must reflect.* (Quran 14: 25)

*And the similitude of a bad saying is as a bad tree, uprooted from upon the earth, possessing no stability.* (Quran 14: 26)

*Allah created you from dust, then from a little fluid, then he made you pairs, the male and female. No female beareth or bringeth forth save with His knowledge. And no one groweth old who groweth old, nor is aught lessened of his life, but it is recorded in a Book. Lo, that is easy for Allah.* (Quran 35: 11)

*And We revealed the Scripture unto thee only that thou mayest explain unto them that wherein they differ and as a guidance and a mercy for a people who believe.* (Quran 16: 64)

*Say: Each one doth according to his rule of conduct, and thy Lord is best aware of him whose way is right.* (Quran 17: 84)

*They will ask thee concerning the Spirit. Say: The Spirit is by command of my Lord, and of knowledge ye have been vouchsafed but little.* (Quran 17: 85)

*And We have not sent thee O Muhammad save as a bringer of good tidings and a warner unto all mankind, but most of mankind know not.* (Quran 34: 28)

*It is revealed unto me only that I may be a plain warner.* (Quran 38: 71)

*Then eat of all fruits, and follow the ways of thy Lord made smooth for thee. Their cometh forth from their bellies a drink diverse of hues, wherein is healing for mankind. Lo, herein is indeed a portent for people who reflect.* (Quran 16: 69)

*But seek the abode of the Hereafter in that which Allah hath given thee and neglect not thy portion of the world and be thou kind even as Allah hath been kind to thee and seek not corruption in the earth. Lo, Allah loveth not corrupters.* (Quran 28: 77)

*Lo, Allah enjoineth justice and kindness, and giving to kinsfolk, and forbiddeth lewdness and abomination and wickedness. He exhorteth you in order that ye may take heed.* (Quran 16: 90)

*Say: The Holy Spirit hath revealed it from thy Lord with truth, that it may confirm the faith of those who believe, and as guidance and good tidings for those who have surrendered to Allah.* (Quran 16: 102)

*And afterward We inspired thee Muhammad, saying: Follow the religion of Abraham, as one by nature upright.* (Quran 16: 122)

*And We have enjoined upon man concerning his parents. His mother beareth him in weakness upon weakness and his weaning is in two years. Give thanks unto Me and unto thy parents. Unto Me is the journeying.* (Quran31:14)

*Turn not thy cheek in scorn toward folk, nor walk with pertness in the land. Lo, Allah loveth not each braggart, boaster.* (Quran 31: 18)

*Be modest in thy bearing and subdue thy voice. Lo, the harshest of all voices is the voice of the ass.* (Quran 31: 19)

*And whosoever disbelieveth, let not his disbelief afflict thee, O Muhammad. Unto Us is their return, and We shall tell them what they did. Lo, Allah is aware of what is in the hearts of men.* (Quran 31: 23)

*So let not their speech grieve thee O Muhammad. Lo, We know what they conceal and what they proclaim.* (Quran 36: 75)

*This is a Scripture that We have revealed unto thee, full of blessing, that they may ponder its revelations, and that men of understanding may reflect.* (Quran 38: 30)

*Lo, We have revealed unto thee O Muhammad the Scripture for mankind with truth. Then whosoever goeth right it is for his soul, and whosoever strayeth, strayeth only to its hurt. And thou art not a warder over them.* (Quran 39: 41)

*Whoso doeth right, it is for his soul, and whoso doeth wrong, it is against it. And afterward unto your Lord ye will be brought back.* (Quran 45: 15)

*And if two parties of believers fall to fighting, then make peace between them. And if one party of them doth wrong to the other, fight ye that which doeth wrong till it return unto the ordinance of Allah. Then if it returns, make peace between them justly, and act equitably. Lo, Allah loveth the equitable.* (Quran 49: 9)

*O ye who believe! Shun much suspicion, for lo, some suspicion is a crime. And spy not, neither backbite one another. Would one of you love to eat the flesh of his dead brother? Ye abhor that, so abhor the other. And keep your duty to Allah. Lo, Allah is Merciful, Relenting.* (Quran 49: 12)

*O mankind! Lo, We have created you male and female and have made you tribes and nations that ye may know one another. Lo, the noblest of you in the sight of Allah is the best in conduct. Lo, Allah is Aware, Knower.* (Quran 49: 13)

*Allah hath not assigned unto man two hearts within his body, nor hath he made your wives whom you declare to be your mothers, your mothers, nor hath he made those whom you claim to be your sons, your sons. This is but a saying of your mouths. But Allah sayeth the truth and He showeth the way.* (Quran 33: 4)

*And Allah hath heard the saying of her that disputeth with thee, O Muhammad, concerning her husband, and complaineth unto Allah. And Allah heareth your colloquy. Lo, Allah is Hearer, Knower.* (Quran 58: 1)

*Such of you as put away your wives by saying they are their mothers. They are not their mothers, none are their mothers except those who gave them birth. They indeed utter a lie and an ill word. And lo, Allah is Merciful, Forgiving.* (Quran 58: 2)

*Proclaim their real parentage. That will be more equitable in the sight of Allah. And if ye knew not their fathers, then they are your brethren in the faith and your clients. And there is no sin for you in the mistakes that ye make unintentionally, but what your hearts propose, that will be a sin for you. Allah is Merciful, Forgiving.* (Quran 33: 5)

*O Prophet, if believing women came unto thee, taking oath of allegiance unto thee that they will ascribe no thing as partner unto Allah, and will neither steal, nor commit adultery, nor kill their children, nor produce any lie that they have devised between their hands and feet, nor disobey thee in what is right, then accept their allegiance and ask Allah to forgive them. Lo, Allah is Merciful, Forgiving.* (Quran 60: 12)

*Those are they who will be brought nigh in the gardens of delight. A multitude of those of old and a few of those of later time.* (Quran 56: 11-14)

*On lined couches, reclining therein face to face, there wait on them immortal Youths.* (Quran 56: 15-17)

*With bowls and ewers and a cup from pure spring. Wherefrom they get no aching of the head, nor any madness.* (Quran 56: 18-19)

*And fruit they prefer. And flesh of fowls that they desire. And there are fair ones with wide, lovely eyes, like unto hidden pearls. Reward for what they used to do. There hear they no vain speaking, nor recrimination. Naught but the saying, Peace, and again, Peace.* (Quran 56: 20-26)

*Among thorn-less Lote-trees and clustered plantains, and spreading shade, and water gushing, and fruit in plenty. Neither out of reach, nor yet forbidden.* (Quran 56: 28-33)

*He it is Who sendeth down clear revelations unto His slave that He may bring you forth from darkness unto light. And lo, Allah is Full of Pity, Merciful.* (Quran 56: 9)

*And among us there are righteous folk and among us there are far from that. We are sects having different rules.* (Quran 72: 11)

*Say: Lo, I control not hurt nor benefit for you.* (Quran 72: 21)

*Every soul is a pledge for its own deeds.* (Quran 74: 38)

*Lo, those who give alms, both men and women, and lend unto Allah a goodly loan, it will be doubled for them, and theirs will be a rich reward.* (Quran 56: 18)

*O ye who believe, be mindful of your duty to Allah and put faith in His messenger. He will give you twofold of his mercy and will appoint for you a light wherein ye shall walk, and will forgive you. Allah is Merciful, Forgiving.* (Quran 56: 28)

*And He is the Loving, the Forgiving.* (Quran 85: 14)

*By the night enshrouding. And the day resplendent. And Him who hath created male and female. Lo, your effort is dispersed. As for him who giveth and is dutiful toward Allah. And believeth in goodness. Surely, We will ease his way unto the state of ease.* (Quran 92: 1-7)

*Is not Allah most conclusive of all judges?* (Quran 95: 8)

Siraat-E-Mustaqeem, the most authentic Islamic book written for the purpose of making Islamic precepts easy, enumerates the qualities of a good Muslim borrowed from the Quran, Sura Furqan. Chosen here is a selection below for students and scholars of learning:

> The qualities of the pious and faithful Muslims are that they are not proud, nor walk on this earth arrogantly. When ignorant and illiterate people get into heated arguments with them, they do not get angry, nor employ harsh language. They remember Almighty as their Protector and Sustainer. They expend their wealth carefully and do not indulge in extravagance. They never kill any person except in self-defense. They don't commit adultery, but God forgives those who resolve to abstain from major sins and redeem themselves by doing virtuous acts in future. They never tell lies and are not attracted toward vulgar words or actions. When they recite the holy Quran, they ponder over the text. They do not recite the same as blind and dumb, but try to understand its edicts and guidance given by God. They do not depend upon their own sources of knowledge and capabilities, but seek God's guidance and blessings that could allow them and their children to walk on the path to righteousness.

Selected below are a few excerpts from Hadith Al Bukhari, related by Abu Huraira on the virtues of being a good Muslim:

> The virtue is in reality abstaining from the evil that is why it has been said, to keep away from sins is virtue. If there arises any quarrel or disagreement amongst certain people, one must judge without favor or impartiality. If one sees any obstruction on a path that could cause harm to others, for example a stone that

can hurt or thorns that can prick, to remove those obstructions amounts to great acts of virtue. Be upright and respectful, bear the burden of others, but do not become a burden to others.

Aisha regarding the manners of the Holy Prophet said, his deeds are a living example practical exegesis, amplification and explanation of the conduct enjoined by God. The Prophet said, the good deed that you perform, if it brings peace to you, this action is moral beauty. A human being may be the follower of any religion, but in his mind and thought he has the concept of an outline in which he fills colors by his conduct. Every man in his nature is virtuous, that is why God has implanted in the nature of every man the sense to discern between good and bad, may he belong to any community or follow any religion.

When a delegation of Christians from Najran came to Medina, they enjoyed the hospitality of the Holy Prophet. They were lodged in the mosque and performed their prayers in conformity with their own rites.

A person who rises above his own desires and leaning, while seeing an object, he will be, verily, very close to equity and justice.

Recovering Sharia from the jungles of misconceptions is also a present day dilemma of violence which has nothing to do with Sharia, but with man-made innovation of laws to justify their brutal acts against the fabric of false religion frayed by centuries of distortions. Suicide bombings are one of those ill-starred actions, sanctioned by the zealots while training and bribing the young jihadists with the reward of heaven. Life is a sacred trust between man and God, not to be violated under any circumstances. When someone takes one's own life with the intention of destroying countless more, one commits a heinous crime not sanctioned by the Islam. The Quran and the Hadith forbid suicide and killing of non-combatants.

*Slay not the life which God has made sacrosanct unless it be in a just cause.* (Quran 6:151)

*And kill yourself not, for God is truly merciful to you.* (Quran 4:29)

Prophet Muhammad speaking against the extremists said, "Perished are the hair-splitters. Perished are the hair-splitters. Perished are the hair-splitters."

*If you avoid the most heinous of prohibited conduct, We shall conceal all your sins and admit you to a gate of great honor.* (Quran 4:31)

Mohammad Hisham Kamali said, "There is no place in Sharia for arbitrary rule by a group or a single individual

Muhammad Rashid Rida says in response to a question whether a formal constitution was Islamic and whether any objectionable elements therein invalidated the whole of constitution:

> If a constitution seeks to establish a good government, defines the limits of power and ascertains the criteria of accountability, then it would be in harmony with Islam. Should there be an instance of disagreement with any of the principles of Islam, only that element should be addressed and amended. For after all many of the great works of human interpretation of Law also contain errors, but this does not invalidate the whole of the endeavor or manual in which such an error might have occurred.

# Chapter 10 ~ Sharia in Knowledge Enshrined

*Read in the name of thy Lord Who created. He created man from a clot. Read and thy Lord is most Honorable, Who taught to write with pen, taught him what he knew not.* (Quran 96: 1-5)

The very essence of Islam lies in attaining knowledge and striving toward disseminating its import so that goodness could be the only criteria to benefit oneself and the mankind. The first challenge for Muhammad, the man, to become Prophet began with the advent of gaining knowledge and understanding its divine power in order to stay afloat in the ocean of love, empathy, kindness and compassion. Noble in character and loving by nature, when he became the recipient of the holy revelations, his virtues of humility, justice and harmony were honed to such pure brilliance that he could not harm anyone even in his thoughts. The staunch proponent of peace and equality, he made the acquisition of knowledge a priority which could bestow upon his followers the gold of reason to distinguish between right and wrong.

*And We sent not as our messengers before thee other than men whom We inspired. Ask the followers of the Remembrance if ye know not!* (Quran 16: 43)

The word used for scholastic theology—kalam is like Sharia, the common term for the Law, late in making its appearance. This does not mean that there were no early Islamic theology. Rather both Law and theology were at first comprised in the term fiqh—human interpretation of Law, which embraced right action and right belief. Fiqh contrasted with knowledge, which applied chiefly to the gathering of Hadith, history and biography. When it was desirable to make a distinction between fiqh as theology and fiqh as Law, the expressions, insight in religion, and insight in knowledge, were used. The latter term recognizes the close bond between right action—the Law, and Hadith—vehicle of the Sunna.

The elaboration of theology was greatly accelerated in Islam by the political and social history. During the first two centuries, more than one segment of the Islamic community separated from the main body, at times taking up arms against those who differed. Thus made intensely aware of boundaries, it became necessary for Islamic thinkers to state what the boundaries were. One of them was Abu Hanifa who wrote The Fiqh Akbar 1. John Alden Williams

Here are some of the titles of articles written by Abu Hanifa:

"We do not consider anyone to be an infidel on account of sin, nor do we deny his faith."

"We enjoin what is just and prohibit what is evil."

"What reaches you could not possibly have missed you, and what misses you could not possibly have reached you."

"We disavow none of the companions of the Apostle of Allah, nor do we adhere to any of them exclusively."

"We leave the question of Ali and Uthman to Allah, who knoweth the secret and hidden things."

"Insight in matters of religion is better than insight in matters of law and knowledge."

"Difference in the community is a token of divine mercy."

*The Bedouins say: we believe. Say, O Muhammad: you have not believed, say rather, we have become Muslims.* (Quran 49: 14)

Another thinker by the name of Abu Mansur al-Maturidi skilled in interpreting Quranic verses gives the interpretation of the verse above in relation to understanding knowledge: "Islam is knowledge of God without modality and its locus is the breast. Faith is knowledge of Him in His Godhead, and its locus is the heart inside the heart, within the breast. True worship of God is knowledge of God in His Unity and its locus is the innermost heart."

*They believe that God knows universals, but not particulars. This too is plain unbelief. The truth is that there does not escape Him the weight of an atom in the heavens or in the earth.* (Quran 34:3)

The famous theologian Al Ghazali uses the verse above to impart knowledge to Muslim Community. He says, "It is customary with weaker intellects thus, to take the men as criterion of the truth and not the truth as criterion of the men. The intelligent man follows Ali who said: 'Do not know the truth by the men, but know the truth, and then you will know who are truthful. The intelligent man knows the truth, then he examines the particular assertion. If it is true, then he accepts it, whether the speaker is a truthful man or not, for he knows that gold is found in gravel with dross.'"

The Holy Prophet made it incumbent on those who came to him to seek knowledge to impart the same to others. And desired even those who were considered to be in the lowest strata of society to be uplifted to the highest level through education. (h.4). Islam, in fact, lays the basis of mass education, education of men as well as women, of children as well as adults. The Holy Prophet himself made arrangements for the education of women (h.5). Writing was encouraged (hh.5-9) and acquisition of knowledge was made the standard of excellence (h.10). It is spoken of in the highest terms of praise (hh.11-14), and this explains the insatiable thirst for knowledge of the Muslims of earlier days. H. 15 The Holy Prophet makes it incumbent upon every Muslim, man or woman, old or young, that he/she should acquire knowledge, and thus introduces the principle of compulsory education. A warning is given that when a nation gives up the acquisition of knowledge, its downfall is sure. (h.16). Maulana Muhammad Ali

*And say, O my Lord, increase me in knowledge.* (Quran 20: 114)

*And whoever is given knowledge is given indeed abundant wealth.* (Quran 2: 269)

*Allah will exalt those of you who believe and those who are given knowledge to high degrees.* (Quran 58: 11)

*Then exalted be Allah, the True King! And hasten not O Muhammad with the Quran ere its revelations hath been perfected unto thee, and say: My Lord, increase me in knowledge.* (Quran 20: 114)

*Then whoso doth good works and is a believer, there will be no rejection of his effort. Lo, We record it for him.* (Quran 21: 94)

*Doing good to beasts is like doing good to human beings. Cruelty to animals is forbidden just like cruelty to human beings.* (B & M. Msh 6: 7)

Acquisition of knowledge was integral part of the Prophet's household, especially for the wives of the Prophet Muhammad. The

Prophet's wives were poets and scholars in their own right, and jurists by default since they were exposed to the Prophet's conduct of justice as the head of the Muslim community. Aisha the youngest wife of the Prophet became proficient in poetry, literature, Arabic history and genealogy. After the death of the Prophet she was a source of guidance to the Muslim Community, proficient in interpreting the revelations and skilled in relating the examples of the Prophet's dealings in matters lawful and unlawful and duties fair and obligatory. Her knowledge in medicine was impeccable and she discussed the remedies of the various illnesses with foreign delegations who came to see the Prophet. She was considered a great scholar in giving advice concerning the sayings of the Prophet to be collected for Hadith. Two thousand two hundred and ten sayings of the Prophet recorded in Hadith are attributed to Aisha. She had excellent memory, even the Caliph Omar sought her advice when he had difficulty in understanding any juristic problem.

Another wife of the Prophet by the name of Safiyah was well versed in the interpretation of the juristic law. She had a group of women from Kufa under her tutelage, also teaching them the benefits of the hygiene and maintaining good family relationships.

Umm Salmah, another of the Prophet's wife was endowed with the wisdom and intellect. She exerted such great authority in interpreting revelations that many men scholars used to say, why we should turn to others when we have the Prophet's wives to consult.

Aside from the Prophet's household, more and more Muslim women in Mecca and Medina became interested in learning and teaching others. A few of those are mentioned below.

Rabiah from Medina learned the art of making decisions on legal issues on the basis of revelations with candid judgment to such a high degree that many male scholars came to her for advice and implementation of the revelations.

Umm Atiyyah mastered the science of Islamic jurisprudence, attracting the scholars from Basra for her input on some issues, both complex and difficult.

Aisha bint Saad was so learned on the authority of the Prophetic Traditions that famous jurists and scholars became her pupils.

Sayyida Nafsa was a later Muslim scholar who excelled in Shafi School of Islamic Law and attracted illustrious students.

Umm Ad-Darda was a great theologian herself and an expert on the writings of Al Bukhari.

Fatima bin Qays was so grounded in the knowledge of juristic wisdom that even the Caliph Omar could not challenge or change her views.

Umm Salim, the mother of Anas imbibed the Prophetic Traditions with such candor and passion that her reservoir of knowledge could not be exhausted.

> The science of Law is the knowledge of the rights and desires whereby man may fully conduct his life in this world and prepare himself for the future life. The Sharia was not erected into a formal code, but remained, as it has been a discussion on the duties of Muslims. Though Law was not quite separate in conception from Duty, and never became fully self-conscious. This characteristic determines the nature of the judgment passed upon various activities which goes back to the basic conception of a divine legislation mediating absolute standards of evil and good. The majority of actions do not come within the scope of Law at all, since the initial principle of liberty assumes that in the absence of revealed information about an action, it is morally and therefore legally indifferent. The remainder are either good or bad in themselves, but in both cases the Law recognizes two categories, an absolute and a permissive. Thus the full scheme comprises of five classes: Actions obligatory on believers. Desired or recommended, but not obligatory actions. Indifferent actions. Objectionable, but not forbidden actions. Prohibited actions (H. A. R Gibb).

"Part of glorification of God is respect for the elderly and for the one who knows the Quran by heart without being fanatical about it or deviating from it, and respect for holders of authority who are just," the Prophet Muhammad said.

Some of the Muslim Caliphs following the Prophet's death tried their best to treat everyone with justice and shun fanaticism. One of the caliphs, Caliph Omar, after conquering Jerusalem gave the patriarch of Jerusalem a treaty which is still honored by the tolerant Muslims.

In the name of Allah, the Merciful, the Compassionate. This is the covenant which Omar ibn al-Khattab, the servant of Allah, the Commander of the Faithful grants to the people of Allah, the Holy House. He grants them security of their lives, their possessions, their churches, their crosses. They shall have freedom of religion and none shall be molested unless they rise up in a body against us. They shall pay tax for the protection of their caravans during their journey from the city toward their destination and their lives and properties would be safeguarded.

Later conquests landed Muslims into Spain as far as France. Berber Arabs known as Moors ruled Spain and were also called Veil Wearers, because the Berber custom of men going veiled. During that time the Arab world made astounding advances in medicine, chemistry, astronomy, mathematics, engineering, agriculture and in the fields of art and literature, excelling in research and innovation.

The Jews, Muslims and the Christians in the Middle East lived in harmony to their common Judaistic heritage. They agreed that the world was one, that the material universe was the visible Cloak of God.

So the Muslim Arabs began mining the knowledge of past civilizations, especially the Greek. The Greeks had left their wisdom in manuscripts, which lay hidden in the dust of the monasteries. Some Nestorian monks realized their value, gathered the Greek writings and fled to Persia. The Arab scholars helped them translate the ancient wisdom of the Greece into Arabic.

Much of the translation was done at the great Baghdad House of Wisdom, founded by the Caliph Mamoun in Year 803. For approximately three centuries this was the world's greatest center of learning. The whole schools of linguist-translators and other scholars flocked to this center. Mamoun appointed Nestorian Christian scholar Hynanyn ibn Ishaq at the head of this academy. Hynanyn in return employed the Jewish, Muslim and the Christian scholars to translate wisdom of the worlds.

The Arab researchers used their Arabic language and worked within Arab culture at Baghdad, their first priority was to study the

Greek philosophers in order to develop rationale for religious truths. The Sunnite Muslims in power at Baghdad made much of the Islamic doctrine of consensus. Agreement constituted truth, even if the Quran had to be questioned.

The entire book of Sharia is only one line: Love God's creatures as you would love God.

# Chapter 11 ~ Sharia Intoxicated Groups

"Islam recognized Jews, Christians, Zoroastrians and later Hindus as People of the Book, that is, as having a written Scripture which has come from God, and as such they should become protected minorities within the Islamic State." Marmaduke Pickthall

Drunk by the rivers of wine, milk and honey, the authors of zeal have succeeded in bribing young Muslims with a first class ticket to the heavens for killing men, women and children. The only way to stop these lunatics from luring young and innocent Muslims into the barbaric practices of rape, murder, stoning, and decapitating is to shut down all schools of education where hatred is inculcated blatantly and where they are brainwashed into promoting evil as virtue and killing a noble act to gain the reward of heavenly delights. Not just Muslim schools, but even mosques should be closed down where mullahs preach the seven deadly sins of war, hatred, cruelty, malice, bigotry, injustice, and intolerance. Glossing these sins with the glitter of virtues which would pave the way smooth for would-be jihadists, would-be murderers, would-be suicide-bombers, would-be tyrants, would-be misogynists, and would-be ignoramuses to the very gates of the Muslim Paradise where beautiful virgins await their pleasure and where there are rivers of wine, milk and honey to quench their insatiable thirsts?

Shutting down such institutions is only the first step in striving toward gaining love, peace and harmony in the world. The second step is to educate the poor, young, underprivileged victims of zealotry with the knowledge of Islam in all its purity of kindness, compassion, forgiveness, tolerance which is the most noble of messages in all religions without the dross of ritual, dogma and fanaticism. It would be of great benefit for the good to the whole of humanity if scholars, historians, and theologians could put their heads together in convincing the bigots, zealots and extremists to study the Quran and Hadith in the light of the Prophetic Traditions and to follow the example of the Prophet Muhammad's life. The Prophet whom they claim to obey and revere was the living Quran in loving, helping, forgiving and emancipating women from the shackles of injustice and inequality. The third step depends on the success of this arduous mission for each and every Muslim to continue cultivating the kernels of peace and nurturing the precepts of love and rising without fear and with great resolve and courage against all evils of tyranny, zealotry, destruction. Extinguishing the flames of zeal should be incumbent upon all Muslims as is the acquisition of knowledge upon every Muslim, male and female.

For reward and salvation countless atrocities are committed and still being committed by the puppets of piety, belonging to a myriad of violent organizations. A handful of those are selected in this chapter with a hope that the disease of violence could be eliminated with reason, intellect and by active participation in creating peace-loving organizations for generations of would-be peace-activists, working toward peace of the world. Below are a few of the violent groups listed chronologically.

Hezbollah; Hamas; Al-Qaeda; Lshkar-e-Taiba; Taliban; Boko Haram; IS; ISIL; ISIS

## Hezbollah 1982

Hezbollah, meaning The Party of God, is a Lebanon based Shia terrorist group, supporting Palestinian rejectionist groups in their struggle against Israel, also providing training camps for Iraqi Shia militants to attack foreign invaders. This group's headquarters are based in Lebanon, but their cells of operation are scattered worldwide. This group relies on different tactics of bombings, justifying their actions as the defender of Lebanon against Israeli aggression. In April 1983 the group claimed responsibility for suicide truck bombing at the US Embassy in Beirut. Also bombed the US marine barracks in Beirut the same year in October. A year later the group hijacked a TWA Airplane. They attacked Khobar Towers in the Saudi Arabia in year 1996. In July 2006 Hezbollah kidnapped two Israeli soldiers, sparking a war in which they claimed victory. Hezbollah's military chief Imad Mughniyah was killed in February 2008 by a vehicle bomb in Damascus, and the group blamed Israel for their leader's death, threatening vengeance and retaliation. The UN Special Tribunal for Lebanon—STL in July 2011 indicted four Hezbollah members for the assassination of the former Lebanese Prime Minister Rafiq al-Hariri who was killed five year earlier by a car bomb in Beirut. Since then Hezbollah has vowed that they will not allow any of their members to be arrested, accusing STL as a proxy of Israel and United States. Though Hezbollah didn't claim responsibility, a car bomb exploded in July 2012 on a bus in Burgas, Bulgaria, killing five Israeli tourists and a Bulgarian.

August 2014 Hezbollah changed its tactics, defending the Syrian regime and Lebanon borders against the threat of the Sunni IS—Islamic State, emerging as a terrorist organization of ruthless Sunni militants from the mountains of east Lebanon and across Syria to the borders of Iraq and Iran. The new threat posed by IS; ISIL—Islamic State of the Iraq and Levant has direct impact on Hezbollah's decision making by allowing sixteen year old boys to engage in fighting which was initially set as eighteen year old before they could approach the battleground. A string of atrocities and massacres committed by IS in Iraq against the Kurds, Yazidis, Shiites, Christians, Turkmen have jolted Hezbollah to awareness that IS is evil, not Islamic and must be expelled from the territories they have seized in Iraq and across the northern Syria. For Hezbollah fighting continues.

Hezbollah, fighting alongside with the Syrian army in June 2014 in defense of the Syrian President Bashar al-Assad were recalled to Iraq when IS and allied Iraqi groups overtook Mosul. Syrian rebels took advantage of this in strategic Qalamoun area north of Damascus and adjacent to Lebanon's eastern border to mount counter-attacks against pro-Assad forces.

Initially, Hezbollah had spearheaded a campaign from November 2013 to April 2014 to drive away rebels from Qalamoun, but renewed fighting spilling across the border into Lebanon is forcing Hezbollah to battle the Syrians and Lebanese Sunni fighters drawn from an array of factions, including IS; Jabhat al-Nusra—Al Qaeda's Syrian affiliate.

## Hamas 1987

At the beginning of first Palestinian uprising, the roots of Hamas are in the Palestinian branch of the Muslim Brotherhood. It is supported by the Palestinian territories. This group believes that an Islamic Palestinian State be established in place of Israel. It has publicly expressed a willingness to end long-term hostilities if Israel agrees to a Palestinian State based on Year 1967 borders with Jerusalem as its capital. The stronghold of Hamas is mainly along the Gaza Strip and areas of the West Bank. Hamas is an independent group, though getting a minimal support from foreign countries. This group has succeeded in many anti-Israel attacks in Israel and many Palestinian territories. They have conducted large scale bombings against civilians, while planting roadside explosives and launching rockets into Israel. Hamas views Israelis as invaders and considers suicide bombing and mortar and rocket attacks as tools of retaliation.

In June 2008 Hamas entered into agreement of six month truce with the Israel, but after the truce rocket attacks were resumed. Israel launched a fierce attack on December 2008 and after destroying much of the infrastructure in Hamas territory of Gaza Strip, declared a unilateral ceasefire in January 2009. Year 2010 brought a fresh confrontation between the Israel and the Palestine when Israeli Defense Forces intercepted a flotilla of humanitarian aid vessels bound for Gaza Strip. The seizure of one ship led to a violent confrontation, resulting in the death of nine passengers. This incidence was condemned by Hamas as a massacre, appealing to the international activists to end the blockade of Israel since Year 2007 along the Gaza Strip.

## Al-Qaeda 1989

The Al-Qaeda is an offshoot of the Muslim Brotherhood, nurtured a decade before in Egypt and in some areas of the Saudi Arabia. The Arabic word, Al-Qaeda, meaning literally the Base, as in a training base was adopted by Osama Bin Laden to start his militant Islamist group based on Wahhabi interpretation of Islam from the manmade tenants of the Muslim Brotherhood. A staunch believer in the distorted version of Islam, he began preaching global jihad against his version of the infidels, including the Muslims who didn't conform to his strict rendering of the so-called Islamic laws concerning jihad, women, education and jurisprudence.

After a decade of warfare when the Soviets pulled out of the Afghanistan in early Year 1989, Osama found a perfect haven to establish his Al-Qaeda Base in the very hearts of the Afghanis. The Soviets were defeated and the poor, orphaned, underprivileged youths were to be trained as future jihadis by Osama and his teacher Azzam. While Azzam favored internal fighting only in Afghanistan until the true Islamist government was settled, Osama's ambition was to train Al-Qaeda to wage a global warfare. Azzam was killed in the same year as of the Soviet's defeat and Osama became the sole master of the Al-Qaeda. Pressed by zeal, he masterminded several attacks against the military and civilian personnel, gloating over his cunning plans and getting drunk by the very color of hoary scenes and freshly spilt blood. The Al-Qaeda jihadists aided in downing two Black Hawk helicopters in Year 1993, also taking credit for the bombing of the World Trade Center in the same year. Such jihadi Islamists were also responsible for a car bomb that exploded outside a Saudi-US joint facility in Saudi Arabia that was used to train the Saudi National Guard. In Year 1998 the US embassies in Kenya and Tanzania were attacked by the Al-Qaida. The Year 2000 witnessed a strike against the U.S.S Cole in Yemen, which killed seventeen American sailors.

The Al-Qaeda's ideology envisions a complete break from all foreign influences in Muslim countries and the creation of a new world-wide Islamic Caliphate. The members of Al-Qaeda believe that a Christian-Jewish alliance is conspiring to destroy Islam. There are several factions of jihadis inside the folds of Al-Qaeda, amongst them the Salafist jihadists who believe that the killing of civilians is religiously sanctioned, and they ignore any aspect of religious scripture which forbids the murder of civilians and internecine fighting. Amidst the Syrian civil war, the Al-Qaeda factions started fighting each other, as well as the Kurds and the government. Involved in multifarious attacks, the Al-Qaeda ventured an attack on US Embassy in Year 1988. Their boldest attack which shocked the entire world was Nine Eleven Year 2001 on Twin Towers in the New York City, killing more than three thousand civilians.

The Al-Qaeda promotes sectarian violence amongst Muslims. The group is intolerant of non-Wahhabi/Salafi branches of Islam, even denouncing them as infidels. The Al-Qaeda leaders consider mainstream Sunnis, liberal Muslims, Shias, Sufis and other sects as heretics, attacking their mosques and gatherings with any excuse they could procure. Their sectarian attacks include the Yazidi community bombings, the Sadr City bombings, the Ashoura Massacre and the April 2007 Baghdad bombings. In a video message September 5, 2014 Al Qaeeda leader Ayman al-Zawahiri vowed to raise the flag of jihad across the sub-continent as it seeks to exploit the disillusionment felt by the tens of millions of Muslims. He has employed a Kashmiri man by the name of Salim Ahmed to proclaim Al Qaeeda's call to turn India's only Muslim majority state a key battlefield of a new jihad across South Asia. Saleem Ahmed on his little truck parked by his wares on the street by his clothing store in Srinagar's central business district announced, "Ours is not an Islamic war for Umma—a global Islamic nation, it is a struggle for sovereignty over our land and our political right to self-determination."

On September 25, 2014 an Algerian splinter group from Al-Qaeda has beheaded a French Mountaineer Herve Gourdel who was kidnapped while hiking in Algeria. They posted a video online, showing masked gunmen standing over a kneeling Gourdel. They pledged their allegiance to the leader of IS, Abu Bakr Al-Baghdadi and said they were fighting his enemies.

This group calls itself Jund al-Khalifa or Soldiers of the Caliphate, split from Al Qaeda and pledging allegiance to IS

January 7, 2015. Al Qaeda killed twelve employees of French Satirical Newspaper, Charlie Hebdo, wounding eleven, while shouting Allahu Akbar. Allahu Akbar meaning God is Great, Great God sanctioning brutal murders, does that make any sense?

January 15, 2015. Al Qaeda shot dead a woman accused of adultery in Maaret Msinin in Syria. Adulterer shooting adulteress, fair justice?

April 2, 2015. Al Qaeeda linked group al Shabaab attacked Grissa university in Kenya. Four masked gunmen killed one hundred and forty-seven non-Muslim students, including three soldiers and three police officers, sparing Muslim students. The mastermind behind this massacre was Mohammed Mohamud.

**Taliban 1989**

The Talib in Pashto, meaning student, and plural ,students, as in Taliban are Jihadis from the Arabian Peninsula and Mujahedeen—the warlords of Afghanistan who resisted the invasion of Soviet Union in Year 1979, regrouped as Taliban in Year 1989 after the Soviets were defeated, to fight the pro-Soviet Government. The time period is the same as the emergence of Al-Qaeda.

They fashioned their own laws to govern and subjugate. Most of them were orphans or belonging to poor families, the victims of Soviet aggression and taught in madrassas funded by the Saudi Arabia. They were schooled to fight the infidel and brainwashed into believing the distorted version of Islam which had nothing to do with Islam. Trained to have long beards and turbaned at all times, they went from village to village, carrying a copy of the Quran in one hand and Kalashnikov in the other, demanding that the chieftains put down their weapons for the sake of the Quran. If anyone resisted the armed bandits styled as Taliban, they were shot dead on the spot by the Taliban.

The militant Taliban kept fighting the puppet government set by the soviets, but they didn't succeed until Year 1992 when they toppled the government of Najibullah. Yet it was not until Year 1996 that the Taliban kidnapped Najibullah, the president of the Afghanistan, and his brother. They beat both Najibullah and his brother and castrated them publically, dragged their bodies behind a jeep, then hanged them by the wire nooses from the lampposts. After these brutal acts, the Taliban began issuing their man-made edicts of prohibitions outside the pale of Islam. No music, no pool tables, no kite flying, no nail polish, no toothpaste, no television and no beard shaving or adopting the hairstyles of the British or the Americans. The women were to wear burqa, covered from head to toe, and banned from working. The girl schools and colleges were closed.

In early1998, the Taliban succeeded in capturing the northern town of Mazar-e-Sharif. On a spree of blood-thirsty rampage, they slaughtered about six to eight thousands of Shia men, women, and children. Not satisfied with mass murder, they ploughed their way into people's homes, raping, murdering, and slitting the throats of all they could find, regardless of their age, gender or ethnicity. Pressed by the fever of madness, they packed hundreds of victims into shipping containers without water to be baked alive in the desert sun.

Movie theatres were closed and music was banned. The Taliban stopped all women from working in schools or hospitals, and if they deviated from the Taliban's edict of complete covering from head to toe, they were publicly beaten. Local festivities of New Year celebrations were banned, as well as festivities of the two Eids, and Ashura—Shia's Islamic month of mourning. The taking of portraits and photography were banned. At the end of the same year the Taliban, in coalition with their parent group Al Qaeeda's suicide bombers, had launched assaults against America's embassies in Kenya, Nairobi, Tanzania and Dar es Salaam. Their coordinated attacks within eight minutes of each other resulted in deaths of two hundred and twenty-four people and forty-five hundred were injured.

In March of 2001, Taliban blew up two thousand-year old statues of Buddha in the cliffs above Bamiyan and began enforcing more of their man-made laws on the populace of Afghanistan. Religious minorities were ordered to wear tags beginning May in 2001, identifying them as non-Muslims. Hindu women were required to veil themselves in the manner of Afghani women as forced by them earlier. More edicts were enforced in July 2001, banning the game of playing cards. The use of TV, movies, satellite, computers disks, chessboards and musical instruments were prohibited, labeled as unIslamic. In August of the same year eight Christian foreign aid workers were arrested by the Taliban on the charges of preaching, two of them were Americans. A month later, Northern Alliance Commander Ahmed Shah Massoud was wounded in a suicide attack, dying of wounds a few days later.

The most vicious of attacks landed on the American soil was on September 11 Year 2001 by Osama bin Laden as the head of Taliban in coalition with Al Qaeeda. The World Trade Center's twin towers were hit by hijacked planes, killing thousands of Americans in New York. Also, the Pentagon in Washington was attacked.

Malala Yousafzai, a teenager from the district of Swat in Pakistan was shot in the head by Taliban in October 2012 for her courage to promote peace and schooling for girls worldwide. From June to

September 2014, the Taliban had killed seventy-one Afghan National Army soldiers, wounding two hundred and fourteen. They also killed one hundred and fifty-nine police officers, wounded two hundred and nineteen in the Sangin district of Afghanistan. Amongst the Afghan security forces, two hundred and fifty died by the hands of the Taliban in the district of Sangin, the total number of dead and wounded rose to nine hundred in the province of the Helmand.

December 16, 2014

Taliban slaughtered one hundred and forty-eight children in the Army Public School of Peshawar in Pakistan. 'Smallest coffins are heaviest to bear,' writes Dr. Raza in the editorial of Lahore Tribune.

The measure of their atrocities, though endless without retribution, can be summed up in a few lines. The Taliban's network of human trafficking—in addition to raping of the women, abducted them from all walks of life and sold them into sex slavery in Pakistan and Afghanistan. Their harsh edicts forbade women from getting educated. Girl schools and colleges were closed. Women were not allowed to leave home without a male chaperon. They were required to wear a burqa— covering from head to toe and if any part of their body was revealed, they were publicly flogged. One young woman by the name of Sohaila was convicted of walking with a man who was not her relative and charged with adultery. Her body was lacerated by hundred lashes as she was flogged publicly in the Ghazi Stadium. More than six hundred Somali women were abducted, the desirable ones selected for the leaders of the Taliban and the rest carted away in the trucks to Peshawar where they were kept in private homes as slaves or sold into brothels. Women were not allowed to work except in medical profession since no male doctor was allowed to examine a woman.

In the town of Bamiyan alone hundreds of men, women and children were executed. Most of the houses were razed to the ground and some used as bases for forced labor. The religious police of the Taliban scouted everywhere to tyrannize women if they dared go out of their homes to work secretly in schools or to operate their beauty parlors, and if caught, they were flogged mercilessly. To raise funds for their hateful enterprises, the religious police began charging tolls from the trucking companies, including the heroin merchants who were transporting their share of the opium to foreign markets.

## Lashkar-e-Taiba 1990

The literal meaning of Lashkar-e-Taiba is, Army of the Righteous. This group was originally formed in the Kunar province of Afghanistan. Their training camps were located in the North West Frontier Province and many were shifted to Azad Kashmir for the sole purpose of training militants to liberate Kashmir from India. Their primary activities are centered on the Kashmir Valley, challenging India's sovereignty over the territories of Kashmir. But now they are most active in South Asia, operating mainly from Pakistan, deeming India, Israel and United States as existential enemies of Islam. They claim that they fight for justice to free the weak and the poor from their oppressors, but preach that it is the duty of all Muslims to fight infidels until the Muslim rule becomes the dominant way of life in the world, which in essence has nothing to do with Islam, but with the tyrannous rule of the tyrants.

Lashkar-e-Taiba became notorious for massacres. In January 1998 this group murdered twenty three Kashmiri pundits in Wandhama. Their attack on Srinagar airport killed five Indians. In another massacre in March 2000, the militants killed thirty three Sikhs in the town of Chittisinghpura in Kashmir, the same year they attacked Red Fort in New Delhi. They attacked the Indian Parliament in Year 2001, targeting both the military and the civilians. The Australian government charged this group for killing thirty-one people in May 2002 in the Kaluchak massacre. Twenty-four Kashmiri pundits were gunned down in March 2003 in Nadimarg. Lashkar-e-Taiba's bombings in Year 2005 in Delhi killed sixty civilians and maimed five hundred and twenty-seven. Their successful blasts in succession in Year 2006 in Varanasi in the state of Uttar Pardesh killed thirty-seven people and eighty-nine were injured. The same year they killed thirty-seven Hindus in Doda massacre in Kashmir. The Year 2006 was the bloodiest for India through the violence of militants, their Mumbai train bombings alone claiming the lives of two hundred and eleven people and four hundred and seven people were left injured. Their Mumbai attack in Year 2008 was bold and brutal, killing more than hundred and sixty-six people on a three day onslaught. They also breed contention between the Shias and the Sunnis and launch bloody attacks in the cities of Lahore and Karachi in Pakistan. In August 2012, Lashkar-e-Taiba hired two teenage boys, twelve and thirteen years old, to launch grenades at a police post in the town of Sopore for the payment of seventeen dollars. This group, aside from its covert means of violence, employs poor, underprivileged children for suicide bombing.

## Boko Haram 2002

Boko Haram in Hausa dialect means education (other than the Quran) is forbidden. They claim to be Muslims, but their version of Islam is as far removed from truth as any terrorist group who have mapped out their own agenda of distortions to murder, destroy, and tyrannize.

Becoming notorious in Year 2014 for abducting almost three hundred school girls, the Boko Haram's roots can be traced since early seventies. Solidly and effectively organized in Year 2002, its roots sprouted in 1970 with the rise of a preacher by the name of Mohammad Marwa whose sermons were an ocean of madness, rising on the rungs of extremism. He was so vociferous against the Western culture in Nigeria, preaching hatred against the western influence, that he was dubbed as Maitatsine, meaning, the one who damns. Civil war ensued in Year 1980 in the city of Kano when the followers of Maitatsine began rioting against the government. The aftermath of this civil war was that four thousand people were killed, including Maitatsine.

A Muslim cleric by the name of Mohammed Yusuf became the leader of this group in 1990 in the capital of the northeastern state of Borno. The Boko Haram had recruited two hundred militants by Year 2003 and had boldly attacked police stations in the state of Yobe, near the Niger border. Six years later they launched massive attacks against police in the states of Borno, Kano, and Yobe. They killed scores of police officers, but the military task force attacked them in return, leaving more than seven hundred Boko Haram men dead and their mosque destroyed. Their leader, Mohammed Yusuf, was captured, later dying in police custody. His deputy, Abubakar Shekau, reportedly died in this uprising. The same year the Boko Haram militant, Sanni Umaru, released a statement claiming to be the new leader.

In the late summer of Year 2010 the Boko Haram released a video in which Yusuf's deputy, Abubakar Shekau, who allegedly had died the previous year, claimed to be the leader of the group. The same year the Boko Haram militants attacked a prison in the state of Bauchi, killing five people and releasing more than seven hundred inmates. On the day of the President Goodluck Jonathan's inauguration in 2011, the Boko Haram detonated three IEDs near a military barracks in the city of Bauchi, killing ten people. The same year Boko Haram issued a warning to the Muslims. *To avoid Christians, public servants and public buildings and anything related to the politics. This is a government that is not Islamic. Therefore all its employees, Muslims or non-Muslims are infidels.*

One month later the Boko Haram attacked a police station and two banks in the city of Gombi in Adamawa, killing twelve people. The same month they attacked the United Nations compound in Abuja, a car bomb killing twenty five people and injuring more than seventy five. Two months later they attacked Yobe, Damaturu, and Borno states, utilizing IEDs, attacking eleven churches and markets, resulting in a death toll of more than one hundred. January 2012 the Boko Haram sent a shock wave of coordinated attacks against the police, military, and prison in the city of Kano in Kano state, killing more than two hundred people. Six months later the Boko Haram began peace talks with the government of Nigeria. Their spokesman, Abu Qa Qa, warning the media about making any more claims: "We are telling the government to understand that if it is not ready to embrace Sharia and the Quran as the guiding book from which the laws of the land derive, there shall be no peace. And media should understand that for us there is no difference with those fighting with guns and with the pen."

In April 2013, President Goodluck Jonathan stated that he has appointed a team to explore the possibility of amnesty for the Islamist militants. Shekau responded in an audio statement: "Surprisingly the Nigerian government is talking about granting us amnesty. What wrong we have done? On the contrary, it is we that should grant you pardon." The same month the Boko Haram battled with the multinational security forces from the Niger, Nigeria, and Chad in the city of Baga in Borno State, causing more than two hundred deaths, including civilians. Two months later Boko Haram targeted churches in various states on three Sundays, killing more than fifty people. September 2013 the Boko Haram gunmen dressed in military uniforms staged a fake checkpoint near Benisheik in Borno, executing travelers and burning vehicles, causing the death of approximately one hundred and forty-three people.

The Boko Haram militants opened fire in January 2014 in a market in Kawuri in Borno, killing at least forty five people. A month later they torched houses in the village of Konduga, killing twenty three residents. April 14, 2014 the Boko Haram militants kidnapped approximately two hundred and seventy nine teenage girls from a boarding school in Chibok in Borno. In May 5, 2014 the leader of the Boko Haram, Shekau in a video statement declared: "I abducted your girls. I will sell them in the market, by Allah, there is a market for selling humans. Allah says I should sell. He commands me to sell. I will sell women. I sell women."

Hundreds of the Boko Haram militants on May 13, 2014 stormed three villages in the state of Borno. June 3-4, 2014 the Boko Haram militants raided the state of Borno, death toll rising from four hundred to five hundred. Three days later they kidnapped at least twenty young girls over a weekend in northeastern Nigeria in the village of Gakin Fulani. A week later, holding the village Kummabza in Borno state hostage for four days, the Boko Haram abducted sixty women and children, killing thirty men in the raid. August 25, 2014 the Boko Haram, after seizing the town of Gwoza, followed a group of fleeing men disguised as women. They tied the hands of all those twenty men behind their backs and shot them on the roadside, throwing their bodies into a nearby trench and exclaiming: *By the Grace of Allah we have seized the town of Gwoza.*

Shekau in late August announced that Boko Haram wanted to establish an Islamic caliphate, along the lines of the IS group in Syria and Iraq. Fleeing residents have reported that hundreds of people are being detained for infractions of the extremists' version of strict Shariah law in several towns and villages under their control (Springfield-News).

Boko Haram in news November, 2014

MAIDUGURI, Nigeria (AP) — With a malevolent laugh, the leader of Nigeria's Islamic extremists tells the world that more than two hundred kidnapped schoolgirls have all been converted to Islam and married off, dashing hopes for their freedom.

"If you knew the state your daughters are in today, it might lead some of you—to die from grief," Abubakar Shekau sneers, addressing the parents of the girls and young women kidnapped from a remote boarding school more than six months ago.

"The issue of the girls is long forgotten because I have long ago married them off," Shekau says with a chortle. The extremist fighters have ordered girls to stay out of Western-style schools and get married."

Boko Haram is a nickname meaning "Western education is sinful" in the Hausa language.

An earlier video in May showed some of the kidnapped girls, including two explaining why they had converted to Islam. Unconfirmed reports have indicated the girls have been divided into groups and that some have been carried across borders, into Cameroon and Chad. There also have been reports that they were forced to marry fighters who paid a nominal bride price equivalent to twelve dollars.

In a new video released late Friday night, the Boko Haram leader also denies there is a cease-fire with the Nigerian government and threatens to kill an unidentified German hostage.

"Don't you know we are still holding your German hostage (who is) always crying," he taunts. "If we want, we will hack him or slaughter him or shoot him."

A German development worker was kidnapped at gunpoint in Gombi, a town in Nigeria's northeast Gombi in July. Police reported he was ambushed as he drove to work.

In the new video, Shekau wears a camouflage tunic and pants and the black and white flag of al-Qaida is by his side. He is flanked by masked and armed fighters standing in front of four military pickup trucks mounted with anti-aircraft guns. Boko Haram has looted many weapons and vehicles including armored cars from Nigeria's military.

The military has several times claimed to have killed Shekau, and says any new videos are made by a look-alike. But the United States has not removed a seven million ransom on the head of the extremist leader.

October 17, 2014

Nigeria's military chief, Air Chief Marshal Alex Badeh, announced that Boko Haram had agreed to an immediate cease-fire to end a five year insurgency in which thousands have died and hundreds of thousands have been driven from homes in northeast Nigeria. And government officials said they expected the Chibok girls to be released any day.

But Shekau denies in the video that he has agreed to any truce and says he is dedicated to fighting and dying a martyr's death to guarantee him a place in paradise.

"You people should understand that we only obey Allah, we tread the path of the Prophet. We hope to die on this path. Our goal is the garden of eternal bliss," he says.

January, 2015

A great massacre by Boko Haram in Nigeria, killing thousands.

Nigeria, a country divided since its inception and with no strong leadership, became a fertile ground for the Boko Haram who don't even know what is Sharia. Their knowledge is limited to their distorted version of understanding. It spells out as the Law of hatred, tyranny, murder, brutality, intolerance and destruction.

## IS, ISIL, ISIS 2003

IS—Islamic State—the Height of Absurdity, is a pandemonium carved out of the militant groups called ISIL—Islamic State of Iraq and Levant and ISIS—Islamic State of Iraq and al-Sham, referring to the historical Levant, including both Syria and Lebanon. IS emerged from one-time branch of the Al Qaeda in Iraq. Nothing Islamic about this state since they mutilate the meaning of Islamic state which promotes the cause of peace and reconciliation, but they have replaced it with the customs of stoning women, honor killing, raping young and old, hating God's creatures, beheading remorselessly, disrupting the peace of God's creation and murdering innocent men, women and the children.

Where does in the Quran it says to defile the sanctity of holy life by burying alive their victims as they did in the northern Iraq, blind and deaf to the heartrending torments of their live victims. Also in Syria, after seizing eight villages between Aleppo and Turkish border, they killed hundreds of residents, torching their houses and slaughtering indiscriminately.

Amidst countless atrocities, the beheading of an American journalist James Foley August 2014, the beheading of another American journalist Steven Sotloff September 2014, and the beheading of British aid worker Alan Henning October 2014, they send a wave of shock and a chilling reminder that these men must be controlled before they become the plague of mankind, systemic and incurable. January 2015, two Russians shot dead by a Muslim youth at the command of IS Jihadists.

To eliminate the danger of this murrain spreading in future on global scale, we need scholars, not just soldiers and scientists for its demise and eradication. One scholar has already risen up to the occasion, Saudi Arabia's Grand Mufti Sheikh Abdulaziz, the highest religious authority in the country, denouncing the evil acts of the militants by saying, "IS and Al-Qaeda are number one enemy of Islam and not in any way part of the faith." More scholars like him need to rise up to issue fatwas and denounce any militant tyrant who adds to the suffering of the human beings. The suicide bombings in August 2014 in Afghanistan and NATO soldier stabbed to death in Kabul plead the sympathy of more scholars, not only to denounce these murderers, but to churn out authentic knowledge of peace, equality, justice and tolerance to teach these heathens the true precepts of Islam.

The Grand Mufti of Saudi Arabia again spoke October 4, 2014 after the Hajj from Nimrah mosque at Mount Arafat, close to two million Muslims from around the world, "… to hit hard IS with an iron hand the enemies of Islam." Then addressed the pilgrims with much passion:

IS has declared a Caliphate, straddling Iraq and Syria where they have committed a spate of atrocities including beheadings and crucifixions. Your religion is threatened, your security is threatened. These criminals carry out rapes, bloodshed and looting. These vile crimes can be considered terrorism and their perpetrators have nothing to do with Islam. They are tyrants.

IS originated between Year 2003 to Year 2006 in Iraq, supported by Al-Qaeda in Iraq (AQI) and the Islamic State of Iraq (ISI). In October 2006 Al-Rashid al-Baghdadi along with Al-Misri headed the Islamic State of Iraq. Both these leaders were killed in US-Iraqi operation in April 2010. After their deaths, Abu Bakr al-Baghdadi assumed the leadership of ISI, expanding his organization into Syria and in April 2013 adopting the name of ISIL. Later he renamed it ISIS—S meaning sham in Arabic in the context of global jihad in the region of Levant and or Greater Syria. On June 29, 2014 Abu Bakr al Baghdadi assumed the role of the Caliph, naming his caliphate Islamic State. His spokesman al-Adnani described the establishment of the caliphate as, "a dream that lives in the depths of every Muslim believer."

Abu Bakr al-Baghdadi was born in Year 1971 in the city of Samarra fifty miles north of Baghdad. He earned a master's degree and a PhD in Islamic studies from the University of Baghdad in Adhamiya in the suburbs of Baghdad. In March 2003 when the United States invaded Iraq, Baghdadi was still a student and was not thought to be connected to either Al Qaeda or its local offshoot in early years of resistance. Within a couple of years after the invasion he was arrested as a suspected mid-ranking figure in the anti-US Sunni insurgency. He was imprisoned at camp Bucca, the US-run detainment center in southern Iraq.

While detained by US, Baghdadi was not assigned the compound fourteen where the extremist Sunnis were kept. He was considered unremarkable. Finally, when Baghdadi walked out of the US detention camp in Year 2009, he told his captors, "I will see you guys in New York."

In 2014 Baghdadi stepped out of the shadows of the Middle East, but he is a master of large organization, ISIS. His organization is wealthy, the key source of revenue is the smuggling of oil from the oil fields it controls in Iraq and Syria. Baghdadi is known as the invisible sheikh because he covers his face with a veil.

More like a nightmare, ISIS is the twenty-first century cancer in the breast of the entire world, the legacy of several avatars of the extremists in promoting zeal, violence, destruction. Styled as jihadists, ISIS accumulate wealth by robbing banks, exhorting money from kidnaping, even demanding money from truck drivers and threatening to blow up the businesses of the rich merchants if they didn't pour funds into their coffers to sustain their jihadi activities. Their main revenue comes from the illegal sales of oil from oil refineries they have captured. In May 2014 ISIS raided a village in Syria, killing at least fifteen civilians and six children. They succeeded in capturing Mosul airport in June 2014, during that time more than one thousand civilians were massacred in cold blooded executions in the northern Iraq. The capture of a portion of Iraq by ISIS in June was accompanied by brutal crimes against women, raping, kidnaping and at times publicly stoning them to death on the charges of adultery while the adulterers went free. The gunmen of ISIS then went into the mosques in the presence of the worshipers, proclaiming their self-made laws for their self-styled state of Islam.

Women were to be fully veiled, not allowed to leave their homes unless absolutely necessary. The naked mannequins on display were to be covered, male and female. Punishment for stealing would be meted out with amputation of hands. Christians living in the areas controlled by ISIS were given two choices, either accept Islam as their religion, or pay poll tax, refusal to do one or the other would cost them their lives.

Women are the prime target of ISIS, while many are being raped, many more are committing suicide, fearing the alternative to marry their rapists to escape the threat of honor killings. Shia, and especially Christian women, have been specifically targeted by ISIS as they continue to destroy churches and murder Christians. One woman who didn't want to be converted to Islam received the most horrendous of punishment from the hands of ISIS. The militants tied her hands to the back of a car and her legs to another car, splitting her body into shreds by driving cars in the opposite directions. The members of ISIS are literally putting price tags on the abducted girls and women to sell them as merchandise in major Iraqi cities.

Tens of thousands of Yazidis have fled their ancient homeland of Sanjar against the onslaught of ISIS, burning their homes and slaughtering indiscriminately. One night in August 2014 in a village near northern Iraq, ISIS militants surrounded the villagers under cover of machine guns. Men with long beards, their faces masked and Arabic script glistening on the sides of their heads, they began digging ditches.

With brute force they buried people alive. The month of August in Iraq became the bloodiest, IS emerging forth as Insane Slayers, amongst their many atrocious attacks they attacked a mosque during the Friday prayers and killing sixty four worshippers.

# Chapter 12 ~ Extremists in the News

Sharia in context of extremism is a disease, needing correct prognosis to be cured with a right dose of knowledge for the health of humanity. The summaries of atrocities committed by the extremists in this chapter are, not for the sake of shock value, but for the benefit of future generations, especially young Muslims to contemplate and to learn to respect all religions. Hoping that such naked facts could lend them the understanding that life is a gift from God, not to be spurned by killing and to be killed, but to love and cherish all sanctity in life. History is witness to death and devastation by certain factions of human beings throughout the centuries, but hope never dies that someday we will attain peace.

Yahoo Daily Stories Online is the source of this summary below in chronological order.

June 10, 2014
IS massacred seventeen hundred Iraqi soldiers in the city of Takrit.

June 12, 2014
In a single massacre about fifteen hundred Iraqi soldiers and security officers from the former US Camp Speicher base in Salahuddin province were captured and killed by the IS militants.

August 2014
One hundred and fifty unmarried girls and women, predominantly from Yazidi and Christian communities, were sent to Syria, either to be given to ISIL fighters as a reward or to be sold as sex slaves.

Many places of cultural and religious significance in Iraq were destroyed by IS. They have committed crimes of rape and abduction, staging mass executions and murdering women and children.

August 19, 2014
Since July IS in Iraq have declared a self-styled caliphate straddling the Iraq-Syria border, IS fighters have methodically gone after isolated

government bases in northern and eastern Syria, killing and decapitating army commanders and pro-government militiamen.

August 26, 2014

The top Islamic authority in Egypt, revered by many Muslim world-wide, launched an internet-based campaign challenging an extremist group in Iraq and Syria by saying that it should not be called an Islamic State. Its violent attacks, including mass shootings, destroying Shiite shrines, targeting minorities, and beheadings have shocked Muslims and non-Muslims alike. The Grand Mufti of Egypt, Shawki Allam, previously said, "The extremists violate all Islamic laws and principles and described the group as a danger to Islam as a whole."

August 29, 2014

IS posted a grisly video footage on the internet of scores of bodies heaped in the desert of Syrian soldiers they captured and executed following the seizure of Tabqa Air Base. IS executed at least one hundred and sixty soldiers from among five hundred who had made a desperate bid to escape to government held territory after their defeat last Sunday.

August 31, 2014

The Saudi King Abdullah told the media, "These terrorists do not know the name of humanity and you have witnessed them severing heads and giving them to children to walk with in the street. If neglected, I am certain that after a month they will reach Europe and, and after another month, America."

September 13, 2014

The Kurdish women have been fighting alongside men in the Kurdistan Workers' Party to wrest Mount Makhmur in northern Iraq from IS extremists, whose treatment of the women makes the fight especially personal for the female fighters on the mountain. The Kurdish women have fought alongside men for years and can't help being astonished by the fact that IS fighters are frightened by coming face to face with the women. The women fighters also find it amusing that IS men are afraid of them because they believe they will go to hell if they die at a woman's hand.

October 2, 2014

Fred Abrahams, special advisor at Human Rights Watch reports of Yazidi women subject to forced marriages, forced conversions, sexual assault and slavery, and some of those victims were children. Five hundred girls and women of Yazidi communities were given to militants in Syria as reward or sold in markets in Mosul in Iraq and Raqqa in Syria. The militants bought the captured girls, shouting with joy and dancing with their guns.

November 1, 2014

Militants from the Islamic State carried out a mass killing of hundreds of Iraqi prison inmates when they seized the country's second-largest city of Mosul in June, an international rights group said on Thursday.

Some six hundred male Shiite inmates from Badoosh prison outside Mosul were forced to kneel along the edge of a nearby ravine and shot with automatic weapons, Human Rights Watch said in a statement based on interviews with fifteen Shiite prisoners who survived the massacre.

Women and children were said to be among those executed over the past ten days in western Iraq's Anbar province which has been largely run-over by IS

Nineteen Ashura pilgrims near the shrine of Karbala have been killed by IS, attacking Shiites on the Holy Sunday. Like other Sunni extremist groups IS considers Shiites to be heretics and frequently attacks them, especially during their Ashura religious commemorations.

November 3, 2014

IS has slaughtered scores of people from the Abu Nime Tribe. Women and children are amongst those executed over the past ten days in Western Iraq's Anbar Province. IS also killed nineteen Ashura pilgrims near the shrine of Karbala.

November 7, 2014

At the start of the academic year in September, Islamic State revised the school curriculum in areas it controls, eliminating physics and chemistry while promoting Islamic teachings.

Their latest move aims to further reduce the school day into several hours of religious learning at the expense of academic subjects, according to local activists.

"They've announced that they will only teach religion and a little bit of mathematics. Their rationale is that all knowledge belongs to the creator, so even the multiplication table shouldn't be taught," said an activist called Abu Hussein al Deiri.

Islamic State has detained, crucified, executed and beheaded hundreds in recent months in Deir al-Zor for "apostasy", a crime of which it accuses anyone who disobeys or opposes Islamic State.

ISIS claimed credit for twin suicide bombing attacks on two mosques, Badr and al-Hshoosh, during Friday prayers in Sanaa, northern district of Yemen. Death toll rising to one hundred and thirty-seven. Three hundred and forty-five worshipers injured

March 21, 2015

ISIS destroyed ancient Behnam Monastery built by Assyrian King Sauhaib, 4th century near the town of Qaraqosh in northern Iraq.

April 19, 2015

IS released a video showing two groups of captured Ethiopian Christians in Libya being beheaded.

The stories of horrors and atrocities continues into 2016 and who knows for how much longer.

# Chapter 13 ~ Shredding of Sharia

Holy Jerusalem is as sacred to Muslims as to the Christians and Jews, because from that city Prophet Muhammad was ascended to heaven.

During the life of the Prophet Muhammad the word Sharia didn't exist, it evolved as an ongoing code of existence centuries after the death of the Prophet by a succession of caliphs who employed scholars for the benefit of their caliphates to flourish and expand. The Prophet Muhammad's law of Islam was a living, breathing entity by the example of his life, for his actions always followed the path of justice, equality and compassion. For him, revelations comprised a book of learning which could be interpreted a thousand different ways, and as long as he lived he interpreted verses in a way worthy of justice.

If so called Sharia in the hands of the militants is only the instrument of hatred, cruelty, malfeasance, then it needs to be shredded into pieces and tossed into the rivers of past follies where the blood of the countless victims still flows crimson. Even the word Sharia has become an anathema to the whole world, including to the Muslim world who have great horror of extremists dubbed as Islamists. Any law, religious or secular, is fashioned for the benefit of humanity. If it fails in its basic purpose of peace and goodness, it ceases to be a law and is termed as anarchy. Since Sharia has miserably and deplorably failed in its purpose of basic goodness, it has lost its place in the lexicon of Islamic theology in the 21st Century.

Cruelty, injustice, and intolerance have become synonymous with Muslims, murderers, and madmen to such a debilitating extent that even the foundations of Islam are rattling with dread to be crumbled into heaps of dust. In order to save Islam from the throes of devastation, extremists dubbed as Islamists must be stopped.

In order to shred Sharia into neat little strips of understanding one needs to study the lives of the caliphs who assumed the role of making laws using religion as a backdrop to exert their control over Muslims and non-Muslims alike. They were by no means pressed by piety, or driven by passion to do justice, but guided by their quirks, whims and caprice to be kind and cruel in conformity with what they deemed right or wrong. They became the victims of self-righteousness without even knowing that they were setting a precedence for future generations of their actions which would be served as kernels of knowledge to be further corrupted with fresh seedlings of innovation and distortion.

Abu Bakr, the first Arabian Caliph, at the very inception of his rule was more concerned about keeping the Muslim community intact than worrying about the Islamic laws of justice and jurisprudence. Not yet tagged as Sharia it is the future caliphs in succession who would mold and remold their own laws suitable to their power struggle for rule and judgment. Abu Bakr started a string of Ridda Wars—the wars of apostasy, since after the death of the Prophet Muhammad, several factions allied with the Muslims felt the need to formulate their own kingdoms and coalitions, asserting that they were in no way obligated to remain a part of the Islamic community. So the word jihad, which meant inner struggle to fight the evils within oneself during the life of the Prophet Muhammad, was given a new life, the breath of Holy War was infused into is Holy Spirit of peace. Jihad was there to stay for future generations to exploit and tyrannize. Though Abu Bakr's inaugural sermon as a first caliph was mild compared to his frenetic need for expansion to raise the banner of Islam. His sense of humility speaks through his words as he stood before the congregation, saying:

Verily, I have become the chief among you, though I am not the best among you. If I do well, help me, set me right. If I am in the wrong, you shall show faithfulness to me by telling me the truth—to conceal the truth from me is treachery. The weak and the oppressed among you shall be strong in my eyes, until I have vindicated their just rights, if the Lord wills. And the strong among you shall be weak in my eyes, until I have made them fulfill the obligations due from them. Now hearken to me: when the people abandoneth the fight—jihad in the ways of the Lord, He casteth them away in disgrace. Know also that wickedness never aboundeth in any nation, but the Lord visiteth it with calamity. As I obey God and His Messenger, obey me, but if I neglect the laws of God and His Messenger, then refuse me obedience. Arise to prayer, and the Lord have mercy on you!

Abu Bakr's short reign had left behind a trail of blood and ruthlessness not ever seen during the lifetime of the Prophet Muhammad, but there were not enough men to oppose the first Caliph who was a friend of the Messenger of Allah. He was the first one to die a natural death, the latter three out of the four known as the rightly guided caliphs would be murdered most brutally, adding more blood in the wake of Islam as flood of ambition, warfare and expansion. After the death of her father, Aisha the beloved wife of the Prophet Muhammad, stepped forward to portray her father in a favorable light by saying:

When Prophet Muhammad died, the Arabs apostatized and Judaism and Christianity raised their heads, and disaffection appeared. The Muslims became as sheep exposed to rain in a winter's night through the loss of their Prophet until god united them under Abu Bakr.

Adding, she quoted her father as a man of tender spirit, longing for freedom and understanding. Once watching the flight of birds in his garden, he was heard exclaiming:

O bird, you are lucky indeed! You eat and drink as you like and fly, but do not have to fear reckoning of the Day of Judgment. Another time noticing a goat grazing in the field, he contemplated aloud. I wish I were a blade of grass whose life ended with the grazing of any beast, or a tree that would be cut and done away.

The second Arabian Caliph, Omar, also strove toward expanding the dominions of Islam. Since there was no such Islamic Law as Sharia, he ruled according to his own personal code of justice and forgave or punished as his moods dictated. He was made of sterner stuff, claiming no lineage from aristocracy, but behaving like an aristocrat. He appeared calm and unyielding, and prone to violent bursts of temper, he demanded and received obedience. No one loved him, but people had great respect for him. There is a story that Omar once visited the Prophet Muhammad and found the womenfolk chattering excitedly, but the moment Omar appeared they ran behind the curtains and fell into a strange silence. Omar asked angrily why the women were showing less respect to Muhammad than to himself. The Prophet Muhammad laughed and answered, "If the devil himself were to meet you in the street, he would dodge into a side alley!"

Paradoxically the post of the Caliph made Omar mild and gentle and he led an exemplary life of faith, piety, and simplicity. Yet his penchant for control landed on women and he made laws contrary to the teachings of the Prophet Muhammad regarding justice and equality for women and those laws up to this day and age are mistaken as Islamic. To label him as a misogynist would be half true, for though he didn't hate women, he tried to reduce every aspect of liberty from women which they enjoyed during the lifetime of the Prophet. He forbade them to pray in the mosque and tried to forbid them to go on a pilgrimage, besides limiting their activities behind the four walls of their homes. All Muslim women, including the Prophet's wives, had free rein to express their opinions. Omar disallowed this prerogative of freedom of expression, especially in his own household.

At times he could be gentle and forgiving as is apparent from the peace treaty he designed after he conquered Jerusalem. That treaty below was signed by the generals of Omar and by the priests of Sophonius, patriarch of Jerusalem and gifts were exchanged.

In the name of God, the Compassionate, the Merciful! This is the covenant of peace which Omar the servant of God and commander of the faithful have made with the people of Jerusalem.

This peace which is vouchsafed to them guarantees them security for their lives, property, churches and the crucifixes belonging to those who display and honor them. Their churches shall not be used as dwelling houses, nor shall their walls be laid low, nor shall they be damaged in any way. Likewise, the houses attached to the churches, the crucifixes or any other belongings whatsoever. There shall be no compulsion in matters of faith, nor shall they be in any way molested. Nor shall Jews reside with them in Jerusalem.

It is incumbent upon the people of Jerusalem that they pay the poll-tax as other towns do. They must also rid themselves of Greeks and other robbers. Whoever of the Greeks leaves the city, his life and property shall be protected till he reach a place of safety and whoever shall stay in Jerusalem, he shall be protected, but he must pay the poll-tax like the rest of the inhabitants. And whoever wishes to depart with the Greeks, leaving their churches and crucifixes behind, there is protection for them as well. Their lives, property, churches and crucifixes shall be protected till they reach a place of safety.

All that is contained in this treaty is under the covenant of God and His Messenger, and under the protection of the Caliph, and of the believers, so long as the people pay the poll-tax.

Gentle at times, then proud and imperious at other times, Omar could be seen helping the poor and the sick, while laying down the law with a heavy hand for some. The Prophet Muhammad had ordered that the Jews in Khaiber and the Christians in Najran should be allowed full protection. Yet Omar simply disregarded the treaties signed by the Prophet Muhammad and expelled them to Syria, based on his self-made law that only Muhammadens should be permitted to stay in Arabia.

He died as a result of an obscure quarrel over a few pennies. A Persian slave, a convert to Christianity, stabbed Omar one morning when he was entering the mosque, believing he had received unjust verdict from the Caliph.

Uthman became the third Arabian Caliph after the death of Omar. He was accused of nepotism, justly so, for within a decade of his rule all the high offices of the state were in the hands of his close relatives. He was prone to bouts of zeal and piety and had ordered even his brother to be flogged publically for drunkenness, though no such punishment was ever meted out during the life of the Prophet Muhammad. No valid code of Sharia existed during his Caliphate, either, and he invented his own laws to solve the problems of the daily conflicts.

The first copy of the Quran was compiled during his reign and he, too, expended his energies on warfare. Muayiya, the governor of Syria, had written to Uthman that he hoped to launch an expedition against Cyprus, saying that the island was so close that he was being kept awake at night by the barking of the Cyprian dogs. So Uthman launched a navy assault against the Byzantine naval base and Cyprus fell. Next, the armies of Uthman conquered the island of Rhodes. In addition to war booty, they found the remnants of the statue of the Sun-god designed by Chares of Lindos, one of the Seven Wonders of the World. This statue had fallen in an earthquake hundreds of years before. It was cut up and shipped to Syria and nothing more was heard of it except that a junk dealer was reported to have employed nine hundred camels to carry the bronze fragments away.

While the conquests increased the power and prestige of Uthman, there was a source of constant quarrels amongst the army who felt that too great a share of the wealth was pouring into the state treasury. The baggage trains filled with treasures sometimes disappeared on their way to Medina. Even Uthman's revision of the Quran, his chief claim to fame, was derived from a decision made by Omar, with the important difference that Uthman took care that Muhammad's warring expeditions in self-defense to ward off the attacks of the Umayyads were expunged and there was much tampering of the text. Abdallah ibn-Masud announced publicly that the canonical version of the Quran as revised by Uthman was a monstrous falsification. Uthman gave orders that all the copies of the Quran in the provincial libraries should be publicly burned, and since he took possession of the copies belonging to Muhammad's family and destroyed them, his version is the only one that has survived.

Uthman was brutally murdered by several assailants, the chief amongst them Muhammad ibn Abu Bakr. Uthman was reading Quran in his room when the assailants struck him and the copy of the Quran was drenched with his blood.

Ali, finally was chosen as the fourth Arabian Caliph, though he accepted the post reluctantly. His reluctance was based on his personal feeling of doom and presage. Proponent of peace, much like the Prophet Muhammad, he was overwhelmed by rifts and wars in the making. Aisha, the Prophet Muhammad's youngest wife, accused him of being complicit in the murder of Uthman and fought against him, though her army was defeated. Islam, to him, was the embodiment of justice, equality and compassion, so no Islamic laws were designed or implanted during his reign. Besides, he had no time for religious contemplation. He was sucked into wars he didn't like and was heartbroken.

Muayiya, Ali's governor in Syria, was quick to take vengeance after arresting Muhammad ibn Abu Bakr the alleged murderer of Uthman. He had vowed that he would dress him in an ass's skin and burn him alive, but he was so overcome by hatred that he stabbed his prisoner.

Then Muayiya had the dead Muhammad dressed in an ass's skin and burned.

Constrained to besiege Syria and on the brink of victory, Ali was tricked into accepting truce by the treachery of Muayiya and returned to Kufa. Later Muayiya proclaimed himself Caliph in Jerusalem. Ali foretold his own end when one day while leaving his house to go to the mosque for morning prayers he encountered the wailing of geese. One of his servants wanted to chase them away, but he said, "Let them cry, they are weeping for my funeral." As he was wending his way down a narrow passage toward the mosque, he was murdered by a poisoned sword wielded by Abdal Rahman. Ali was taken home, he was alive for three days, forgave his assassin, requesting that he be treated mercifully.

Damascus became the seat of the next caliphs and Muayiya became the first caliph after Ali's son Hasan abdicated his right to the caliphate in favor of Muayiya, since he abhorred war as strongly as his grandfather Prophet Muhammad. During the twenty years of his reign, Muayiya ruled according to his own laws which suited his taste and ambition, so Sharia was non-existent. He, also, adopted the policy of warfare, and his chief battlefronts were against the East, against Africa and against Byzantium. He was known to be gentle and tolerant as well as treacherous. Living in luxurious palaces, he kept himself aloof from religious fervor, but on his deathbed he requested, "Bury me with some hair of the Prophet and a paring of his nails. Then leave me alone with the Most Merciful of the merciful."

After Muayiya's death, his son Yazid became the next Caliph of Damascus. His mother was a Christian by the name of Maysun, and historians tell us that he inherited the gift of poetry from his mother, but also the cultivated ruthlessness of his father. No mention of Sharia during his reign either, but he became notorious for ordering the great massacre of Hussain—the Prophet's grandson and his family on the field of Karbala in Iraq. Thus becoming the author of the great split of Islam into Shias—followers of Ali, and Sunnis the followers of Sunna—living by the example of the Prophet Muhammad's life.

Yazid, pressed by his innate need to rule the entire world, sent large contingents of the Syrian army against the armies of Medina. The leader of those armies was an old general by the name of Muslim. When he conquered Medina, he showed no mercy. For days his soldiers raped, pillaged, and destroyed shrines and buildings. The mosque of Muhammad was turned into a stable, while colleges, hospitals and public buildings were torched. Medina, the home of the Prophet was turned into wilderness. The Syrian army marched on to Mecca, besieging the city. The Kaaba was burnt to the ground, and black stone split into three pieces. Suddenly, Yazid apparently died of consumption and the siege was lifted.

Within one year the three caliphs in succession died, each one of them bringing ruin upon their empire. Finally, Abdal Malik was chosen the next caliph of Damascus. No sight of Sharia during his ten year reign either, for most of his time was devoted on warring expeditions. When asked why he waged wars so mercilessly, he answered, "I enjoy wars! I am weary of being told to fear God." Abdal Malik exclaimed once, "I shall smite the neck of the next person who warns me against God's punishment on the caliphs." His chief lieutenant by the name of Hajjaj was more brutal than the Caliph. On an expedition to Kufa, Hajjaj entered the mosque and terrified the worshippers by his harsh speech, beginning with a verse by the poet, Suhaym ibn Wathil.

I am he that scattereth the darkness and climbeth the heights

As I lift the turban from my face you shall know me.

Then he began histrionically, waving his arms:

O people of Kufa I see before me heads ripe for the harvest and the reaper, and verily I am the man to do it. Already I see blood between the beards and the turbans."

The Prince of the True Believers has spread before him the arrows and the quiver and found in me the cruelest of all arrows, of the sharpest and strongest wood. I warn you if you depart from the paths of righteousness, I shall not brook your carelessness, nor listen to your excuses. You Iraqis are rebels and traitors, the dregs of the dregs! I am not the man to be frightened by an inflated bag of skin, nor need anyone think to squeeze me like dry fig. I have been chosen because I know how to act. Therefore, beware, for it is in my power to strip you like bark from the tree, to pull off your branches as easily as one pulls off the branches of the Selamah tree, to beat you as we beat the camels which wander away from the caravans, and grind you to powder as one grinds wheat between millstones. For too long, you have marched along the road of error. I Hajjaj am a man who keeps his promises, and when I shave I cut the skin! So be there no more meetings, no more useless talk, no more asking, what is happening or what shall we do?

Abdal Malik who loved war, died peacefully in bed. On his deathbed he summoned his son Walid, saying, "Why are you mourning? When I am dead, put on your leopard-skin, gird yourself with sword, and cut off the head of everyone who gets in your way."

Sharia was absent during the reign of Walid and he turned out to be as gentle and ruthless by turns to his enemies as Muayiya. He was gentle toward women, never lost his temper in their presence, but kept Hajjaj in employment against the advice of his wife. He built the first hospice for the blind and an asylum for the lunatics. During his reign his empire stretched from Spain to the borders of china. His armies overran Transoxiana, penetrated deep into India, and in three short years conquered all of Spain. Walid was already on his deathbed when the prisoners of Spain were brought to him. After Walid's death his brother Sulayman succeeded to rule over the vast caliphate. Sulayman's first act of generosity was to release all the prisoners captured by Hajjaj, and his first act of cruelty was against the governor of Spain for some unexplained reason. The governor was deprived of his rank, title and reduced to penury. Sulayman died of plague and was succeeded by his brother Umar.

Caliph Umar of Damascus didn't need to formulate new Islamic laws. He restored to the Jews and Christians the churches which had been taken from them and attempted to conciliate the followers of Ali by restoring to them the oasis at Fadak, which had been the property of the Prophet Muhammad. He reduced the taxes, ordered the horses of the royal stables to be auctioned and deposited proceeds in the state treasury. One day his son remonstrated that ills of the society could be rooted out only by stern measures. To which he replied, "That means the sword, and there are no good reforms which can be accomplished by the sword." He died after a reign of two years.

Next caliph from Damascus was Hisham, a bitter man, raging against his enemies remorselessly. He liked horses more than men and boasted of four thousand horses in his stables. There were uprisings in Iraq and Africa. Corruption was rampant in the provinces of the government. Byzantine armies were surging across Asia Minor. He ruled for almost twenty years and before his death chose his nephew Walid, the son of Yazid II, as his successor.

Walid inherited from his uncle the empire which stretched from the steppes of Mongolia to Morocco, included Arabia, Egypt, Spain and North Africa and most of the islands of the Mediterranean — Majorca, Minorca, Corsica, Sardinia, Crete, Rhodes, Cyprus, a part of Sicily and nearly all the islands of the Aegean. Drunk with the power of wealth and ambition, the Caliph Walid of Damascus went on a campaign to hound the descendants of Ali. When Yahya, the son of murdered Zayd was killed in a battle, his severed head was sent to Walid and he ordered the body of the slain to be impaled on a cross. One day while reading the Quran, Walid came upon a verse demanding all men their total submission to the will of God. After reading this verse he got so enraged that he set up the Quran on the other side of the room and shot arrow after arrow at it until the pages were reduced to tatters. Then, in a fit of madness he wrote down this quatrain.

Dare you threaten me in my proud rebellion?
I am Walid — the most rebellious of men
O Quran when you appear at the Judgment Seat
Tell God who it was who tore you to shreds

Only a year after his profligate rule, Yazid the son of Walid I rose in rebellion. He marched toward Bakhra, south of Palmyra, where Walid was living in a fortress castle. Yazid besieged the castle, saying, "I have come to destroy the most profligate of the Caliphs." The guards of Walid were outnumbered by the army of Yazid, so Walid retired to inner sanctuary with the copy of another Quran as his only protection. His head was cut off and paraded through the streets of Damascus on a spear.

Yazid III became the Caliph of Damascus, the first one born out of a slave mother. Within five months he died mysteriously and was succeeded by his brother, Ibrahim, who reigned only for two months. A dictator by the name of Marwan al-Himar became the next Caliph of Damascus. In Persia, a soldier by the name of Abu Muslim rose to destroy the rule of Umayyads. When his armies advanced toward Iraq and the coasts of Syria, the governor of Khorasan Nasr ibn-Sayyar appealed to Marwan for assistance. Armies of the Abbasids headed by Abu Muslim and armies of the Umayyads headed by Marwan teetered on winning and losing for months, when finally Marwan, as a fugitive in Egypt was felled outside a Christian church, hit by a javelin in the stomach. Later, the Abbasids were able to find sacred relics buried a little way from the church, the mantle of the Prophet Muhammad, his finger ring and staff. These sacred objects fell into the hands of Abul Abbas who called himself as-Saffah or the Shedder of Blood, a new dynasty which was to last for five hundred years. Sharia claimed no place during the power struggle of these centuries in succession.

Umayyads had attempted to destroy all the descendants of Ali, and Abbasids went on a spree of vengeance to destroy even the last vestiges of the Umayyad rule. They invited the Umayyad princes to a banquet near Jaffa, promising amnesty. The banquet had just started when the executioners entered strangling every prince while the hosts kept on feasting. When the daughter of the Caliph Hisham refused to divulge where she had hidden her jewels, she was cut down by the sword. Prince Aban, the grandson of the same Caliph with one hand and one foot cut off, was led through the villages of Syria, while a herald cried, "Behold Aban, son of Muayiya, the most renowned cavalier of the Umayyad House." The Abbasids then dug up the graves of the Caliphs and amused themselves by whipping the remnants of the bodies before putting them to flames. Finding the body of the Caliph Hisham in his robes of state, they gave him eighty lashes of whip as a posthumous punishment. The Prophet Muhammad had spoken of the brotherhood of the faithful, but the Caliphs of Damascus destroyed that by elevating themselves to the ranks of the emperors.

A succession of Abbasid Caliphs became notorious for their cruelty and compassion, as well as their patronage of arts and sciences and of their tolerance for all religions. Their empires flourished despite their excesses in luxuriant living, warring expeditions, interspersed with acts of cruelty. Such savage acts were rare, mostly on an individual basis as a result of pride, anger or a sudden flaring of sadistic streak.

As-Saffah, the Caliph of Baghdad, surrounded himself with the jurists and the theologians. He amused himself by collecting Hadiths, though remained ignorant of Islamic precepts, regarding himself as the incarnation of vengeance of God, a man more than half divine, and a brother to the Prophet Muhammad. With a great show of piety he would don the striped mantle of the Prophet while presiding. Beside his throne stood executioners with the leather mat ready for the head of any victim subject to the wrath of the Caliph. He wrote poetry filled with his lust for blood.

Our swords are dripping with blood, and they have brought vengeance
The great princes of the past brandished them on the battlefield
And heads of our enemies are broken to fragments
Like smashed ostrich eggs

As-Saffah died of smallpox and his brother Al-Mansur became the next Caliph of Baghdad. His twenty years of reign with flourishing of arts were splintered with deceit, tyranny, and violent wars on the road to expansion. His first act of violence fell on Abu Muslim who had helped Abbasids come to power, but acted as if he was more powerful than the Caliph. Al-Mansur lured Abu Muslim to his camp outside the walls of Ctesiphon on the plea that he needed his advice. As soon as Abu Muslim entered the Caliph's tent, the Caliph Al-Mansur accused him of several crimes, ordering his guards to kill him. Abu Muslim struggled in vain and was murdered most brutally. Al-Mansur's greatest achievement was building the city of Baghdad which was completed within four years. During his reign, Baghdad became famous for its musicians and dancing girls, its taverns and market places, its water carnivals and gaudy processions through the streets, its hotels, hospitals and colleges. Great works of Greek, Syriac and Persian were translated into Arabic and Al-Mansur rewarded the translators generously. Despite his sporadic acts of violence, Al-Mansur brought peace to his empire. At his deathbed, he summoned his son Muhammad as his successor, addressing him in the following manner:

Baghdad is a treasure city. Beware of exchanging it for another, for it is your home and your strength. In it I have gathered so much wealth that even if the land revenues were cut off for fifteen years, you will have sufficient for the supplies of your army and for every kind of expenditure.

Muhammad, the next Caliph of Baghdad, assumed the title of Al-Mahdi—the guided one. He opened the prisons of all except of the worst offenders and returned to the few living descendants of Ali the properties confiscated from them. With a vast wealth inherited from his father, he resumed the warring expeditions against the Byzantium. He ruled only for ten years and died while hunting. His youngest son Harun, who had distinguished himself in battles, receiving the title of al-Rashid—the Upright, in rapport with his noble character sent the ring of his father and the Prophet's staff to his elder brother Musa, honoring him as the next Caliph.

Caliph Musa of Baghdad styled himself as Al-Hadi, meaning guide, but had no talent for ruling an empire. Soon Morocco was lost to him, conquered by the grandson of Husain who founded the Idrisid dynasty. There were revolts on the frontiers and uprisings in Arabia and Khorasan and continual wars in Transoxiana. His short reign of unrest and revolts ended when he died suddenly of some nameless illness, succeeded by Harun-al-Rashid.

Historically, Caliph Harun of Baghdad is remembered as the hero of the Arabian Nights, and much like his predecessors, not interested in Sharia. He reveled in luxury and surrounded himself with poets, alchemists, astronomers, and theologians. Aside from spending his spare time in his harem, Harun's favorite pastime was to wander the streets of Baghdad disguised as a commoner in the company of his vizier Jafar, the son of his former tutor Yahya ibn Barmak. For almost seventeen years Harun and Jafar were inseparable, while the Caliph bestowed upon Jafar wealth and honors. It was rumored that the Caliph had homosexual relationship with Jafar. Suddenly, without warning, when Harun returned from a pilgrimage to Mecca, gave orders for the execution of Jafar. Jafar's head was placed on the central bridge of Baghdad and two halves of his body on the other two bridges. After that the Caliph abandoned Baghdad and retired to his summer palace at al-Raqqa.

The reason for Jafar's sudden fall from the Caliph's grace was attributed to the fact that Harun's sister Abbasa was married to Jafar on a condition that they would never stay in the same house and no children were to be born out of this marriage. Upon learning that Jafar had fathered two children out of this marriage with his sister, Caliph Harun was incensed. First the two boys of Jafar were strangled, then Harun's sister murdered, and finally his friend and vizier Jafar executed. After these murders Harun lost interest in kingship and luxuriant living, performing his duties like a sleepwalker. Still prone to excessive rages and after almost twenty three years of his opulent reign, he learned of the rebellion of the Rafi and he marched to the village of Sanabad to subdue the rebellion. He was exhausted by long journey and illness and on the brink of death when Rafi was brought before him as captive. Harun-al-Rashid said, "You have brought me here and you shall pay for it. You shall be killed as no man was ever killed before." The Caliph's orders were obeyed immediately. Rafi was hacked to pieces slowly, and one by one the pieces of his body were thrown at the Caliph's feet.

Muhammad, the son of Harun-al-Rashid, succeeded to the caliphate of Baghdad while his half-brother Abdullah was in Khorasan. Caliph Muhammad is remembered only for his love for luxury and indolence, surrounded by jugglers, dancing girls, and soothsayers. However, from the bowers of his luxurious living, he emerged forth as a war-lord, sending an army of forty thousand troops to destroy his brother Abdullah. It was a political blunder since Abdullah had the best army and defeated the army of Muhammad on the battlefield of Rayy. Then Abdullah laid siege on the city of Baghdad which lasted for fourteen months and half the population of Baghdad was killed. Muhammad was compelled to surrender, was tricked into escaping by boat, but Tahir employed by Abdullah succeeded in sinking that boat. Muhammad swam to the shore, tried to conceal himself in a house, but was followed by the guards of Tahir and cut to pieces, his severed head sent to Abdullah in Khorasan.

The caliphate of Baghdad under the reign of Abdullah flourished to its zenith. He established a Hall of Science at Baghdad with a library and astronomical laboratory. Islam was granted the freedom of expression by reasoning in his court, while he invited men of learning for discussions as diverse of faith as Jewish, Christian, Sabaeans and

Zoroastrian. This was the budding of Sharia for a very short period, not ever again to see the light of its birth in the true sense of the word. Islamic virtue of peace and reconciliation was not to be tainted by zeal and orthodoxy. Islamic justice was to be justified only if followed by acts of clemency. Man was endowed with the power of free will. All things were subject to change, and Quran itself, was far from being the final verdict on human progress. Since man was free to do as he pleased, God was not responsible for the crimes of mankind. Such liberal doctrines were challenged by the fanatics, amongst them Hanbal, who was prepared to fight to death on behalf of the strict interpretation of the Quran. Those interpretations were the lethal weapons of the bigots and the zealots as far as Abdullah was concerned so he continued to rule under the moral codes of justice, clemency, tolerance, and compassion. After twenty-one years of just rule Abdullah died and his caliphate passed on to his real brother Muhammad, the namesake of his half-brother.

Muhammad styled himself as al-Mutasim—the steadfast, but he turned out to be the lord of tyranny, a sadist, and immoral. He moved his court seventy miles away from Baghdad, creating a new city called Samarra. The Christian churches of Egypt were plundered for columns and pavings to decorate his new capital. When a schismatic leader by the name of Barbak revolted, the Caliph sent a large army to defeat him. Barbak was brought to his court as captive. Al-Mutasim commanded that he be stripped naked and die a slow, lingering death. Barbak's one hand was sliced off by the executioner and flung it to his face, then the other hand in the same manner. Then Barbak's feet were cut off while he twisted and kicked in his own blood on the leather carpet, shouting for mercy and beating against his face with his stumps. Finally, his head was cut off to be displayed on the bridge at Baghdad as a warning to the rebellious. Al-Mutasim didn't even know the meaning of virtue or justice, the religion of Islam meant no more to him than it meant to his brutish Turkish guards. He reigned for eight years, shredding the justice of Islam into rags of deeds, knotted with the agony of recollections so very intolerable and unforgivable. Now IS, ISIS, ISIL are trying to outdo what a handful of madmen did in the name of Islam a few centuries ago, planting the seeds of evil, tyranny and destruction.

Sharia, if it ever existed, was shredded into shards of brutal, unimaginable laws of hate, malice cruelty, and still is in throes of being resurrected if it can produce the legal documents of its noble birth. (TheHistory of Islam, Robert Payne).

## Conclusion:

There is no such thing as Sharia. No book of law is written on this subject as a valid document of any historic significance with the exception of man-made laws gnarled with distortions. If Sharia is an Islamic Law, what does it mean? Laws made by men without the shadow of religion are the only laws by which people can be governed in close proximity to justice, equality and freedom. In this world of multiple beliefs, no single religion could enforce its laws to govern people with diverse ethnic, cultural and religious beliefs. Are Jews governed by some Jewish Law on the stage of this world? Or Christians by the Christian Law. Or Hindus by the Hindu Law? Or Sikhs by the Sikh Law? Or Bahia by the Bahia Law? Or Buddhist by the Buddhist Law? Paradoxically, there is only one law by which people can be governed, and that law is the Universal Law of Nature. If so-called Sharia serves as the law of hatred, tyranny and oppression, then there is no room for it in the heart of mankind. If any god tells its creatures, as in the case with IS, to rape, murder, behead, mutilate and destroy, then he/she/it is the false god of madmen and hatemongers, not worthy to be obeyed or worshipped.

Scanty seeds of Sharia planted by the Caliphs were blackened by the congealed blood of the innocent victims. However, the beautiful face of the so-called Sharia can still be recovered if we can peel away layers upon layers of distortions from the ravaged face of the past. If and when we are capable to scrape away all the layers of ugliness, the noble face of Sharia would emerge as nobly reflected by the example of the Prophet's life, promoting love, peace, justice and equality.

**September 25, 2014**

This manifesto was published by Saudi Arabia, available online. More than one hundred and twenty Muslim scholars from around the world joined and wrote an open letter to the militants of IS, denouncing them as un-Islamic by using the most Islamic of terms.

Relying heavily on the Quran, an eighteen page letter picks apart the extremist ideology of the militants who have left a wake of brutal death and destruction in their bid to establish a transitional Islamic State in Iraq and Syria.

Awad said that aim of the letter is to offer a comprehensive Islamic refutation, point by point, to the philosophy of Islamic State and the violence it has perpetrated. The letter's authors include well known religious and scholarly figures in the Muslim world including: Sheikh Shawqi Allam, the grand mufti of Egypt, and Sheikh Muhammad Ahmad Hussein, the mufti of Jerusalem and All Palestine.

The letter includes the following: "It is forbidden in Islam to torture. It is forbidden in Islam to attribute evil acts to God, and it is forbidden in Islam to declare people non-Muslims until he or she openly declares unbelief."

This is not the first time Muslim leaders have joined to condemn the Islamic State. The chairman of the Central Council of Muslims in Germany, Aiman Mazyek told the nation's Muslims that they should speak out against the terrorists and murderers who fight for the Islamic State and who have dragged Islam through the mud.

The Muslim leaders who endorsed the letter called it an unprecedented refutation of the Islamic State ideology from a collaboration of religious scholars. It is addressed to the group's self-anointed leader Abu Bakr Al-Baghdadi, and the fighters and followers of the self-declared Islamic State.

The words 'Islamic State' are in quotes, and the Muslim leaders who released this letter asked people to stop using the term Islamic State, arguing that it plays into the group's unfounded logic that it is protecting Muslim lands from non-Muslims and is resurrecting the caliphate—a state governed by a Muslim leader that once controlled vast swaths of the Middle East.

"Please stop calling them the Islamic State, because they are not a state and they are not a religion," said Ahmed Bedier, a Muslim and the president of United Nations, echoing the speech of President Obama who made a similar point. Referring to Islamic State by one of its acronyms—ISIL, disconnecting the group from Islam. Enumerating its atrocities—the mass rape of women, the gunning down of children, and the starvation of religious minorities— President Obama concluded, "No God sanctions this terror." Below is the summary of the letter jointly written by the Muslim scholars.

**The Letter:**
It is forbidden in Islam to issue fatwas without all the necessary learning requirements. Even then fatwas must follow Islamic legal theory as defined in the Classical texts. It is also forbidden to cite the portion of a verse from the Qur'an—or part of a verse—to derive a ruling without looking at everything that the Qur'an and Hadith teach related to that matter. In other words, there are strict subjective and objective prerequisites for fatwas, and one cannot 'cherry-pick' Qur'anic verses for legal arguments without considering the entire Qur'an and Hadith.

It is forbidden in Islam to issue legal rulings about anything without mastery of the Arabic language.

It is forbidden in Islam to oversimplify Sharia matters and ignore established Islamic sciences.

It is permissible in Islam [for scholars] to differ on any matter, except those fundamentals of religion that all Muslims must know.

It is forbidden in Islam to ignore the reality of contemporary times when deriving legal rulings.

It is forbidden in Islam to kill the innocent.

It is forbidden in Islam to kill emissaries, ambassadors, and diplomats; hence it is forbidden to kill journalists and aid workers.

Jihad in Islam is defensive war. It is not permissible without the right cause, the right purpose and without the right rules of conduct.

It is forbidden in Islam to declare people non-Muslim unless he (or she) openly declares disbelief.

It is forbidden in Islam to harm or mistreat—in any way—Christians or any 'People of the Scripture'.

It is obligatory to consider Yazidis as People of the Scripture.

The re-introduction of slavery is forbidden in Islam. It was abolished by universal consensus.

It is forbidden in Islam to force people to convert.

It is forbidden in Islam to deny women their rights.

It is forbidden in Islam to deny children their rights.

It is forbidden in Islam to enact legal punishments (hudud) without following the correct procedures that ensure justice and mercy.

It is forbidden in Islam to torture people.

It is forbidden in Islam to disfigure the dead.

It is forbidden in Islam to attribute evil acts to God.

It is forbidden in Islam to destroy the graves and shrines of Prophets and Companions.

Armed insurrection is forbidden in Islam for any reason other than clear disbelief by the ruler and not allowing people to pray.

It is forbidden in Islam to declare a caliphate without consensus from all Muslims.

Loyalty to one's nation is permissible in Islam.

After the death of the Prophet, Islam does not require anyone to emigrate anywhere.

In view of the atrocities committed by these Sharia-intoxicated groups, there are a few suggestions for their acronyms.

Boko Haram—Blood Hounds

IS—Ill-starred Stabbers

ISIS—Intolerant Slayers by Iblis Seduced

ISIL—Ignorant Satanic Infidel Lucifer

Such madmen afflicted with the leprosy of the distorted version of Sharia have, ignorantly, much to the benefit of Islam, unraveled the knots of lies hiding the true precepts of Islam. In response to the brutal acts of the militants, the Arab nations have joined hands in digging out the much forgotten truths and exposing them to the sunshine of this new millennium. Foremost amongst them the Prophet Muhammad's pearl of love granting gender equality. The United Arab Emirates has taken a lead in promoting the Prophet's love for justice and equality for women.  Major Mariam Al Mansouri, United Arab Emirates first female air force pilot has joined the coalition against the ISIS.

A welcoming change for the Arab nations in this century twenty-one to bring back the law of Islam as lived by the Prophet Muhammad. Hope is in the air and sky is the limit.  Peace to the world.

Peace to the world seems like a distant dream, but it is with regret and sadness when I conclude this book with a comment that everywhere I look I see Muslims steeped deep in the marshlands of hate, malice, bigotry, hypocrisy.  Close to home even in Springfield Ohio the Muslim community in throes of self-righteousness are concerned about dress code, ritual piety, what to eat, who to associate with, neglecting entirely the message to Islam to help the poor, to visit the sick, to comfort the ones less fortunate and underprivileged.  Even the Imam of the mosque turns a blind eye to the suffering of one family in particular in dire need of sympathy, kindness, counselling.  If charity begins at home then it is the obligation of the Muslim family members to help their kindred.  Sadly the mom of that particular family (whose daughter-in-law and her children are suffering) is deceased, dad is remarried, brothers and sisters don't care, and Muslim community too busy amongst themselves and with their outward acts of piety can't spare a moment to visit the sick mother of the distressed wife, or to offer a kind word to the depressed children.

About the plight of a Muslim family which I couldn't help but write as a closing comment has nothing to do with Sharia, but everything to do with the essence of Sharia, a kind heart with compassion to right the wrongs done to anyone regardless of any religion.  Sharia invented, distorted, reinvented and choked with man-made laws pleads for a breath of fresh air fanned by fair scholars to regulate the rhythm of love, peace, justice and equality.

Not least but last, regretfully and astonishingly even the Muslim women donned in the fabric of false Islam-o-phobia deem hijab Islamic. Lured toward hateful militants, they are late in learning that they are attracted toward ugliness of savage men, abandoning the beauty of Islam marred by the laws both tyrannical and oppressive.

# References

Rahmani, Abdu. Woman in Sharia. Islamic Book Center, 1996.

Williams, John Alden. Islam. George Braziller, 1962.

Ahmad An-Na'Im, Abdullahi. Islam and the Secular State. Viva Books, 2000.

Pickthall, Marmaduke. The Glorious Koran. Alfred A. Knopf, 1992.

Khalidi, Tarif. Images of Muhammad. Doubleday, 2009.

Payne, Robert. The History of Islam. Dorset Press, 1959.

Kritzeck, James. Anthology of Islamic Literature. New American Library, 1964.

Gibb, H. A R. Mohammedanism. Oxford University Press, 1970.

Natiq, Abdul Qayyum. Siraat-E-Mustaqeem. Al-Amin Publications, 1992.

Mushin Khan, Muhammad. Sahih Al-Bukhari. Maktaba Dar-us-Salam, 1996.

Kidwai, Azra. Islam. Lustre Press Roli Books, 1998.

Frager, Robert. The Wisdom of Islam. Godsfeld Press, 2002.

Hashim Kamali, Muhammad. Shariah Law. Oneworld, 2009.

Hefley, James and Marti. Arabs. Christians. Jews. Logos International, 1978.

Armstrong, Karen. The Great Transformation. Anchor Books, 2007.

Helminski, Adams. The Light of Dawn. Threshold Books, 1998.

Cleary, Thomas. The Wisdom of the Prophet. Shambhala Classics, 2001.

Markham, Ian. Blackwell Publishers. A World Religions Reader, 1996.

Saqib, Shaikh Syed. Adam Publishers. Fiqh-US-Sunnah, 1999.

Gairdner, W.H.T. Nice Printing Press. Al Ghazali's Mishkat-Al-Anwar, 2007.

Azmi, Mustafa. Suhail Academy Lahore. Studies in Early Hadith Literature, 2001

Iqbal, Safia. Adam Publishers. Woman and Islamic Law, 2013.

Spencer, Robert. Regency Publishing, Inc. Onward Muslim Soldiers, 1962.

Suharwi, Maulana Makbool Ahmed. Zam Zam Publishers. Four Illustration Imam, 2008.

# About the Author

Farzana Moon is a historian and a playwright. She has a Master's degree in Education, and is well versed in Moghul history and Islamic literature. Two of her previously published books on spirituality are: *Sufis and Mystics of the World*; *Irem of the Crimson Desert*. Her published works on Islam are: *Prophet Muhammad: The First Sufi of Islam*; *No Islam but Islam*. Seven of her published books in the series of the Moghul emperors of India are to be adapted for documentaries. Two recently published in those series are: Bahadur Shah Zafar: Poet Emperor of the Last of the Moghuls; The Moghul Saint *of Insanity*. Currently she is working on a book, The Living Quran.

**ALL THINGS THAT MATTER PRESS**

FOR MORE INFORMATION ON TITLES AVAILABLE FROM
ALL THINGS THAT MATTER PRESS, GO TO
http://allthingsthatmatterpress.com
or contact us at
allthingsthatmatterpress@gmail.com

**If you enjoyed this book, please post a review on Amazon.com
and your favorite social media sites.
Thank you!**